Don'

put us

away

C000174753

To order, or for details of our bulk discounts, please go to our website www.criticalpublishing.com or contact our distributor, Ingram Publisher Services (IPS UK), 10 Thornbury Road, Plymouth PL6 7PP, telephone 01752 202301 or email IPSUK.orders@ingramcontent.com.

Don't put us away

Memories of a man with learning disabilities

CRITICAL
PUBLISHING

Richard Keagan-Bull

Foreword by
Mel Giedroyc

First published in 2022 by Critical Publishing Ltd

All rights reserved. No part of this publication may be reproduced, stored in a retrieval system, or transmitted in any form or by any means, electronic, mechanical, photocopying, recording or otherwise, without prior permission in writing from the publisher.

The authors have made every effort to ensure the accuracy of information contained in this publication, but assume no responsibility for any errors, inaccuracies, inconsistencies and omissions. Likewise, every effort has been made to contact copyright holders. If any copyright material has been reproduced unwittingly and without permission the Publisher will gladly receive information enabling them to rectify any error or omission in subsequent editions.

Copyright © 2022 Richard Keagan-Bull

British Library Cataloguing in Publication Data
A CIP record for this book is available from the British Library

ISBN: 978-1-915080-41-7

This book is also available in the following e-book formats:
EPUB ISBN: 978-1-915080-42-4
Adobe e-book ISBN: 978-1-915080-43-1

The rights of Richard Keagan-Bull to be identified as the Author of this work have been asserted by him in accordance with the Copyright, Design and Patents Act 1988.

Cover and text design by Out of House Limited
Project Management by Newgen Publishing UK
Printed and bound in Great Britain by 4edge, Essex

Critical Publishing
3 Connaught Road
St Albans
AL3 5RX

www.criticalpublishing.com
Printed on FSC accredited paper

CONTENTS

PART III. BECOMING A CHAMPION

PART IV. BELONGING

PART V. MY NAME ON THE DOOR

REVIEWER COMMENTS

This is an honest and at times poignant book filled with humour. Richard's stories of love and international travel, of finding meaningful work and true belonging are gripping. I couldn't put it down...

Baroness Sheila Hollins

It has been an absolute privilege to get to know Richard since I was elected as his MP in 2015; he is a truly remarkable man with a very special gift of advocacy. Richard's book is moving and funny, and it is really important. Far too often the voices of disabled people are overlooked and ignored by those who make decisions that affect them. Richard writes so clearly about his extraordinary life, and in doing so he speaks powerfully about the experiences of disabled people and the importance of creating a society where everyone is valued, cherished and supported. This book should be read by policy makers, politicians and community leaders everywhere.

Helen Hayes MP

ABOUT THE AUTHOR

Richard Keagan-Bull

Richard Keagan-Bull is a much-travelled man known for his powerful self-advocacy for people with learning disabilities. Famous for his sense of humour and his ability to name things as they are, he does not hesitate to speak his mind to those in power! He is a long-term member of L'Arche, a community which provides him with support and friendship. He was included in the 2021 Shaw Trust Disability Power List of the 100 most influential disabled people in the UK. Richard currently works as a research assistant at Kingston University.

FOREWORD

I was both delighted and honoured to be asked to write a foreword for Richard's beautiful book. I know from experience how challenging it is to write one and reading Richard's, my immediate reaction was *'he has smashed it!'* He brings you his life story, with all its rollercoaster moments – its joys, its flaws, its frustrations, its celebrations – with such honesty and immediacy that you feel you are right there at his side, living it with him. This is the greatest gift that a writer can possess, I believe. To connect with your reader instantly and take them with you on your journey.

Richard allows you, the reader, to see the world through the lens of a person with a learning disability, and it is an eye opener. From the nuts and bolts of everyday challenges to Richard's more philosophical and political thoughts about the world we live in, he writes with honesty and clarity about it all. He has a particular talent for getting to the nub of everything, be it a person, situation or concept. His relish for life is infectious and utterly affirming, and his sense of humour had me laughing out loud. I will not forget the tin of peaches incident, nor the trip to Bob Marley's tomb, for a long time! I particularly enjoyed reading about his travels abroad, his forays into the world of work, and his amazing journey towards getting that precious and elusive thing which we all strive for in life – independence. His insight into social care in this country is fascinating; I was on tenterhooks with Richard when he describes a Lambeth Council meeting where he is forced to wrest the microphone from a nabob and just tell it like it is.

Richard's message is simple: if the government cuts vital funding for supporting people with learning disabilities, it will only lead to a more fractured community. And a fractured community leads to its detriment. This is what I think is at the heart of Richard's book. As human beings we are not and should not be alone. This is a book which celebrates community. Be it family, school, college, workplace, his wide circle of friends, the community of L'Arche or church, Richard shows us how essential it is to feel part of one. Not just as a box to be ticked, but as a real and important beating heart of one. I could go on, but I won't say anything as eloquently as he could, so I will stop.

This is an important gem of a book. I really look forward to reading the sequel, Richard.

Mel Giedroyc
Actress, comedian and television presenter

ACKNOWLEDGEMENTS

I would like to say thank you to my mum and dad for their support and help over many years of being there for me. I want to thank my brother, Philip, who has been a good brother to me.

I also want to thank Vi Hallam, our next-door neighbour, who helped my mum so much when we were young.

I want to thank Dr Hugo Liebeschuetz for believing in me and my brother, and for his support at the children's centre when we were younger, and all the staff, physios and occupational therapists there. He helped us to be who we are now.

I would like to thank Trueloves, the school I went to in Essex, the Thomas Delarue School in Kent and the Derwen College in Shropshire where I spent many happy years. A special thank you to all the staff there.

Thank you to L'Arche where I am now and who support me to live independently to live in my own flat.

I would like to thank everyone at Plough Studios where I used to do my cleaning job, and all at Kingston University where I now work.

I would like to say thank you to the Lambeth Assembly, which I helped to set up, and People First and Walsingham Support, who I enjoy being a trustee for.

I want to say thank you to Hazel Bradley for doing all the hard work over a number of years in typing after listening to me telling all my stories. We've laughed a lot and had fun.

I want to say thank you to Mel Giedroyc for kindly agreeing to write a foreword to my book, and to Irene Tuffrey-Wijne for writing the introduction and all her support. And thank you to the members of my circle of support who have helped me in so many ways: Jacek Drzewinski, Tim Spargo-Mabbs, Maggie Fergusson, Jane Abraham, Chris Asprey, Archana Parmar, Hazel Bradley.

Finally, a big thank you to Di Page and all at the publishers who very kindly agreed to publish my life story. It's exciting! I can't believe my life story is actually going to be published. Who would have thought 50 years ago I would be where I am now.

INTRODUCTION

PROFESSOR IRENE TUFFREY-WIJNE

An ordinary man has written an extraordinary book.

When Richard Keagan-Bull was born with learning disabilities, his mother was told he would never do anything and was advised to put him away (thankfully, she ignored it and became his life-long rock and inspiration, cheering him on). In a rollercoaster of riveting chapters, Richard tells the story of his life in his own unique voice. Starting with his birth and early years, when he was rubbished by the headmaster who threw his schoolwork out of the window, he ends almost half a century later, when the boy who would never do anything landed a job at a university as a researcher on my team.

Richard introduces us to a rich cast of family, friends, teachers, people who support him, and a fascinating selection of characters with walk-on parts. He takes us from the special needs school where disabled boys like him were made to use a wheelchair (despite his legs being perfectly fine) to his first independent shopping trip where he let himself be talked into buying a questionable pair of trousers. He shows us his road towards independence, his pride in having made it into the big wide world when he moved into his own flat at the age of 35, supported by the L'Arche community in London. From there, there is no stopping him. He discovers his gift for standing up and saying it as it is. He becomes a spokesperson for people with learning disabilities in L'Arche UK, and indeed in L'Arche worldwide, as the first chair of the National Speaking Group. It takes him all over the world, with acute observations of the differences between living in India and living in the UK, both pricelessly funny and profound. '*How much we take for granted*', he reminds us. He becomes an advocate with People First, grabbing the microphone out of the hands of the local politician to tell them in no uncertain language what will happen to people with learning disabilities if their funding is cut.

I could go on. Richard's stories left me breathless. They are in turn hilarious, deeply sad, angry and profound. I wanted to grab hold of some of his statements and shout them from the rooftops. He had me laughing out loud, crying into my hanky and back to laughing, sometimes in the space of a single page. That is a rare achievement. I defy anyone to read about his visit to Auschwitz and not be moved to tears.

In sharing his memories so eloquently and in so much detail, Richard has not only told the story of his life, but the history of people with learning disabilities in the UK. He really does speak for people with learning disabilities everywhere. Crucially, he shows us not only what happened to him (from not being free to live relationships in the way you want to having to fight for the support you need) but also how that feels, from the inside. I cannot overstate how important it is for all of us to hear this, because his history is not quite history yet. We need to listen and learn from the reflections of this ordinary man on his extraordinary life, because the attitudes and practices that have shaped so much of that life are still evident today.

In telling his story, Richard has shown us that ordinary people are, in fact, extraordinary – and that everyone is worthy of a place in this world. While there is still a long way to go before that place is taken for granted, Richard gives us a beautiful glimpse of what can happen when we build a truly inclusive society. He gives us hope.

This book deserves a very wide readership. I know Richard's many friends are queueing up to read it, but I believe this should also be read by politicians, policy makers, anyone working in learning disability services and anyone interested in how we can build a better world. You, reader, are in for a treat. I will end this introduction with one of Richard's sentences that I wanted to shout from the rooftops:

It doesn't matter if you're black or white, if you can speak or if you can't speak – it's what you can give that counts.

Thank you, Richard, for giving us so much of yourself. I, for one, am changed by your book. I hope it contributes to changing the world.

Irene Tuffrey-Wijne

Professor of Intellectual Disability and Palliative Care (Kingston University London) and long-term member of L'Arche London

PART I

GROWING UP

CHAPTER 1

MY FIRST MEMORIES

My mum had me at home, at one in the morning, with the cat, Smoky, on the bed. That's what my mum said. I'm the youngest in the family. My mum said if I had been born first there would only have been one in the family. I think I let my presence be known, I did! I think that the day I was born, they never forgot it.

My Granny Keagan was upset because my dad went round to say she had a grandson but she wanted a granddaughter and she never let me forget that. She was upset because she had two grandsons and she wanted a granddaughter. She was more fond of my brother than me.

I think that in the early days my Granddad Keagan found it hard, just because of the kind of person that he was, to cope with my brother and I but as I got older he got very fond of me and so made up for my granny. Don't get me wrong, she was fond of me. But my granddad was more fond of me, he was.

I was born in Barbara Close, Rochford, Essex; I can't remember the number now. I was born at home, and my brother Philip was. I was born on 5th September 1971.

The geneticist said to my mum about me and my brother, 'Put them away. They'll never do anything'. You can't say things like that to my mum! She's a fighter, she is. She would fight for my brother and me till her last breath, she would!

But thank you Dr Lieberschultz, the paediatrician, for having faith in me and my brother.

My mother trained to be a nurse, but part of her training was to be a midwife so she did deliver a few babies. My father was a fruit farmer. He's retired now. He grew apples and pears. My other granny and granddad lived on the farm, they did, but I didn't really know my granddad well. All I really remember is that he was a very tall man. He was diabetic, Granddad Bull, he was. He died when I was really young. I remember him going into hospital. I remember my mother picking me up from school and the ambulance was there, it was, yes.

Mum, 1953

Dad

Great Brays Fruit Farm

My Granny Bull we called little gran, we did, because she was quite little, she was. She was an interesting character. She had a condition; she was paranoid schizophrenic, she was. She could be a very nice character then she could go to being really very horrible to my dad and mum. I don't think she was often horrible to me and my brother, but she was to my mum and dad.

Philip, Granny Bull and me

She would say that my mum wasn't good for my dad. She quite often turned people against people. But as she got older it sort of burned out of her. She turned into a nice granny, she did. When my mum and dad were due to get married, they were supposed to move into the farmhouse and then she changed her mind and my poor mum had to quickly find a bungalow to live in. That was the house in Barbara Close. Granny and granddad lived in the farmhouse and my dad had to commute from the bungalow to the farm every day to work, he did.

Left to right: Auntie Hilda, Auntie Betty, Auntie Flora and Great Aunt Lou

Can I tell you about another character in my family that played a great part in my life? My Great Aunt Lou. Her proper name was Louise but we called her Aunt Lou. She was my granny's sister, my mum's mum, Granny Keagan, her sister. She was a maiden lady. She married her job. She was deputy matron at Southend Hospital, she was. She lived with two ladies, she did. I came to know them as Auntie Betty and Auntie Flora. My brother and I used to go and spend a week in the summer with them in their house in Leigh-on-Sea. She didn't like children very much, she didn't, but tolerated us. She was born in the age when children were seen and not heard.

I never remember her working; she was retired by the time I was born. We used to go and stop with her for a week. My memory of going to stop with her was that we used to arrive complete with our bed linen. We had to take toys to play with. We were quite young. She would make us welcome, she would make us feel welcome but Auntie Betty would do things with us. Auntie Flora would put us to bed and get us up in the morning. She was trained to be a children's nurse. That's what she used to do in the hospital. She told us stories. Auntie Betty did the breakfasts, she did. It was a standing joke; Auntie Lou would still be in bed. We would all climb the stairs to get her out of bed. We would shake the bedcovers and say, *'Auntie Lou, it's time to get up'*. And she would say, *'Oh get out of here!'* She used to come down and we would have breakfast together. We used to go out with her for a walk in the morning while Auntie Betty and Auntie Flora did the housework and then we would all go shopping.

My brother and I used to go next door to a friend of my aunt's called Auntie Winn. We went with Auntie Lou to watch TV (we watched *Crossroads*) because Auntie Betty and Auntie Flora didn't like watching TV; they just liked watching sport. In the afternoons we had dinner. My brother and I used to go for a week together but as we got older we went on our own so we had the whole week to ourselves, we did. I remember when I used to go, Auntie Lou said, *'Auntie Bettie and Auntie Flora will go in the back room to sleep and you and I will go in the front room to play'*. But she would fall asleep and I was left on my own.

Me and Philip as toddlers

With Aunt Lou

Me and Philip in the garden of our Granny

We used to play when they woke up. I played doctors, I did. I was the doctor and they would come in the room and I would tell them what was wrong with them, I did. We would have tea and then later on we had supper and then we went to bed. They walked down the road with us. Auntie Betty would hold one hand and Auntie Flora would hold the other hand. And we walked to see my great aunt and ran up to her.

Years later, my mum and I went to tell Aunt Lou that I was hoping to live in L'Arche (which you can read about in Part II). Her last words to me were, '*As long as it is nice and that the people are nice and you won't be bored, it will be good*', she said. I haven't been bored in L'Arche! I've been very busy! My wish is that she could have come to see the L'Arche community but she died six months before I came to the community. She died at the good old age of 96.

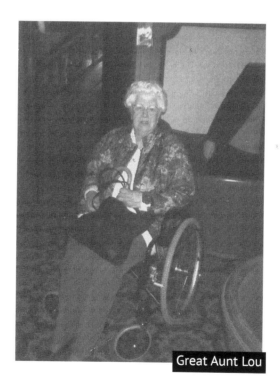

Great Aunt Lou

Granny and Granddad Keagan
at their house in Jersey

I have got a vivid early memory of my Granddad and Granny Keagan –
an embarrassing one! On a Thursday afternoon my mum would take
my brother and I to the children's centre at the hospital and I think
we went for speech therapy and OT (occupational therapy) and all
that stuff, yes. On the way home she used to stop for shopping. One
Thursday we were shouting, 'Granny, granny, granny!' Granny Keagan
and granddad were in the shop. We recognised the car, I think. Granny
Keagan turned round to granddad and said, 'Why are those children not
in control?' I don't think she was very pleased by the noise. We might
have been five at the time. Then she saw that it was us, and I think
she was quite pleased, she was, seeing my mum there as well. In the
end, we all did our shopping together. Granddad paid for us to go

on the toy machine outside the shop. We all went back, one of us in mum's car and one of us in granddad's car, and we all had a drink. It turned into a regular thing, it did.

I remember one summer Granny Keagan sat on a deckchair and it went through, it did! She ended up on the grass, she did, and we all laughed!

Granny Bull, dad's mum, died in 1995 at the age of 93.

Me at a Children's Centre before starting school

With my family. I'm standing at the front

CHAPTER 2

MY FIRST SCHOOL: PAGLESHAM, 1976

The first school I went to was called Paglesham. It was the local village school, it was, yes. I think I went there from about four or five until I was eight. I have a picture of me being at the school, I have. What I remember of it, I didn't like it very much! I met my first girlfriend there, I did, Ann. I think that she was about five. We were very young, we were. She had black hair.

I think that the headmaster – he was a bit of a bully he was, yes. If you didn't get your work right he used to hit you, he did. He used to bully you and pull you by the ears – not just me but the other children as well. He belittled you by what he said.

I remember things like going swimming with the school. We went once or twice a week. We took a long time getting changed and the other children would be ready but me and my brother were a little bit behind. They used to wait for us but the headmaster would call out, '*Come on, hurry up, hurry up!*' and the other children used to laugh.

Years later I met an old classmate who asked me '*Do you remember when the headmaster threw your work out the window?*' I said I didn't remember but this incident remembered by my classmate fitted in with my memories of the head. It has made me want to tell my story. My work is worthwhile and valuable.

I did remember another time involving this same classmate. We were just mucking around in the playground. It was break time and I think that we got into a few scrambles and into gangs and I sort of got in the way, I did. I don't think it was all done on purpose but I ended up upside down and I got my arm broken. I wasn't quick enough to get out of the way.

I must admit that on that day the headmaster was quite a nice headmaster. He ran out of the school to see what had happened. There used to be a lady who watched what was going on in the playground. The headmaster picked me up and carried me into the school because

I was in quite a lot of pain, I was. He laid me down, he did, in his sitting room. He said they would ring for my mum and dad to get me to the hospital and if they couldn't get them they would ring for an ambulance. They got hold of my mum and dad and they took me to the hospital. My poor brother was left at the school. He must have been worried about what was going on. Poor Philip saw a lot of things going on, he did!

I remember another thing that happened at the school. We played football in the school. I used to fall over and the headmaster who was the ref walked on top of me – or over me at least. You could make a comedy out of my life! I wonder how I must have looked then with National Health glasses with wiry bits at the back to keep them on. I must have looked a right somebody, a right idiot, a right carry on!

Tug of war at Paglesham

One afternoon in the week, we went to another school. I think it was to prepare the children in my school to go to the upper school. One day because I used to not get my work right, my girlfriend Ann very kindly did some of my schoolwork for me, she did. The headmaster found out that it wasn't my work and me and Ann had to stay at our school for the afternoon because he found out she had done my work for me. Our relationship didn't last very long because we had a fight. It was over a camera. One of us ended up with a black eye. I can't remember which one of us it was!

I just have to tell you a little thing about Ann. Everyone at the school felt very sad about my Ann. Ann had a younger brother. He wasn't quite old enough to join the school, he wasn't. One day in the term time, I guess it was a sunny day but I can't remember, my mum came to pick us up from school but got stopped by the police. She said she was coming to pick us up but the police said a little boy had gone missing. She went straight to some other families from the school and they were talking and it turned out to be Ann's little brother. Someone went to the family house and Ann's dad said that Ann's mum had had a funny turn and had murdered him. He said they were just trying to find out where she had put him.

It was about five or six years later this woman turned up at Barbara Close where we were living and I shouted it out that it was Ann's mum who murdered Ben and all the neighbours heard. That was quite a hard thing, it was. A few weeks before he disappeared, I went to stop with them, I did, so I suppose it could have been me as well. I don't suppose so really.

Shall we move on to a light-hearted story now at my next school?

CHAPTER 3

MY SECOND SCHOOL: TRUELOVES, 1979

School photo at Trueloves. I'm sitting on the floor in the middle

When I was about eight, after having my arm broken at school, the headmaster and my parents thought that I couldn't cope with going to another normal school. It wasn't working very well and I would get a lot more behind with work. So I went to this lovely school called Trueloves. It was originally built for someone's girlfriend but it all fell through and that was where the name came from. It was all boys, a boarding school for children with special needs. It was in Essex. It was a Shaftesbury Society School.

A lot of the boys there had muscular dystrophy. And they had 15 boys there altogether. It was a nice little school. Even though it was a special needs school, they were still quite strict with us. But one of the things that I liked was that on a Friday night we used to have fish and chips or chicken and chips brought in for us to eat. The weekends were nice because we had breakfast in bed, we did. I shared a room with two other boys because we were the youngest, we were. We used to watch Saturday morning TV, we did. The head of the school, as in the man who was in charge of the evenings and the weekends, the warden, Mr Eden his name was – he could blow hot and cold sometimes, he could. And Matron, his wife, she could blow very hot and cold when she wanted to! Mr Eden was in charge of breakfasts and Matron was in charge of making sure we were behaving ourselves.

I'll just name the boys I used to share a dormitory with: their names were James and then there was Tim. Very sadly, Tim left the school, he did, to go to a new school. Then a boy called David came in and shared the dorm with us. I'll just explain sometimes in the night that James, who used to have trouble moving round in the bed at night, called me to help me move his legs. I had to help him sometimes in the mornings. He liked to get dressed before the care staff came in. So I used to help him with jobs and he sometimes read letters and cards for me that I got from people, and helped me write things. Sometimes I went to his house, I did. He lived on a farm like we did but they were bigger farmers than we were.

Sometimes at Trueloves, Sainsbury's the shop, they bought things for the school, they did, like TVs and nice things like that, and took us out for day trips to Southend-on-Sea and brought a vanload of food for us to eat. Our eyes got so big when we saw the food.

Philip, Dad and me

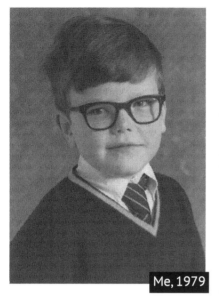
Me, 1979

I guess because of the time, because we are going back 40 years or so now, they insisted when we were going out that my brother and I had to go in wheelchairs. My mum and dad were right, we didn't need the wheelchairs, we could use our legs – but it was the times then. And when we left Trueloves, or when Trueloves closed, the school gave us the wheelchairs and my mum and dad tried to give them back but they wouldn't take them back, so they were put in a corner out of the way and we used them later in life for my granny and granddad and friends of ours who got old.

Me and Philip with Missie, our dog

Trip of a lifetime

I'll just tell you about a holiday we went on with the school. We went on three holidays with the school, all paid for by a local charity I think. One holiday we went to Holland, and the second holiday we went to France but I'll tell you about the third holiday. It was called the 'Trip of a Lifetime' and we went to America – two weeks to Florida. It has to be explained that a lot of the boys at the school because of their disabilities would be lucky to live to the age of 16 so for them it *was* the trip of a lifetime.

Mr Eden told us all the things that were going to happen. The footballer Trevor Brooking, who played for Chelsea, was going to come to wave us off. And the night before we left, the day pupils at the school all stopped the night at the school, they did, because we had to leave early in the morning on our own private plane. I think there were some other people but we were treated like VIPs, I know that. I can't remember how many people went but all the teachers at the school and all the carers and the people who raised the money for us came with us. We left early in the morning and London taxi drivers had paid for some of us to get to the airport.

I remember being on the plane and watching *Rocky* the movie, which had just come out, and hearing 'Kids in America'. That song means a lot to me because we were kids in America going on holiday. We arrived in Atlanta and while we were waiting for the next plane, we were rushed into our own VIP room while everyone else was waiting and we were given lemonade and coke. There was a great big window and the airport staff said they were waiting for two Concordes to come into land, a British Concorde and a French Concorde, and we would be able to see them as if we were in first-row seats. The plane that took us to Florida came to where we were. We didn't have to walk to the plane, the plane came to us.

One of the trips we did we went to Cape Canaveral. We were taken up to see the space shuttle. It was just starting to go on countdown. We didn't see it take off. I can't remember too much of what we did but we went to Disney World in Florida one day and we did lots of swimming in the pool. I remember we all bought pretend guns, we did, and we pretended to be cowboys and Indians. I think we drove the staff in the hotel mad that day, and the people stopping there as well! That's all I can really remember of that holiday in America. I was about nine I think then, or ten.

Me on an American cop's motorbike with Philip and my mum behind: LA, 1981

The year before I went to America with the school, Trueloves, my mum and dad took my brother and I to America, but we did not know then that we would go to America with the school the next year, so I guess my brother and I are two very lucky boys. Granny and Granddad Keagan came to the airport, Heathrow I think it was, and that time Philip and I did have wheelchairs just at the airport because it was quicker to get us to the planes. But Granny Keagan got all emotional when she saw us leaving, thinking she might never see us again. That was her; she used to get very emotional and I think I am very like her.

I used to like the TV show *Chips* about two American cops that used to be on motorbikes. I don't know how she did it but my mum wrote to an American police station and arranged for my brother and I to meet a real American policeman on his motorbike. He came and met us, he did. We had a look around his bike, we did. I think we went to the police station as well, we did. That was a good memory, that was. But my mum and dad also insisted that my brother and I did some schoolwork as well each day.

I have a good memory really, don't I?! The only thing I am not sure about is dates and things.

Cubs and Scouts

Another memory I have of Trueloves is we used to have a Cub and Scouts troop. The Scout leaders came to the school and we put Gang Shows on. Matron and Mr Eden and the carers and the headmaster and the teachers helped us practise what we had to do. One weekend when my brother and I went home, my mum and dad helped us to practise a song that we were going to sing and we got it word perfect. I was going to sing one bit of the song and my brother the other bit. The night of the Gang Show arrived. All our families were coming to see it, and our friends. There was my mum and dad, my granny and granddad and some friends of theirs. And my mum was so proud because she helped us to get the song word perfect. There was four of us singing the song. It was called 'Four Little Fellows', I think. Philip, my brother, sang his bit. I repeated what my brother sung and forgot what I was meant to be singing. All I remember is the people who were helping us behind the curtains whispering the words I was meant to be singing and my poor old mum who had told her friends sitting there that we had been working on it and we had got it word perfect.

Another funny story about the Scout and Cubs pack at Trueloves. One evening we were having a meeting, we were. I was quite new at the school. I think the rest of the boys knew what was going to happen next, but the Scout leader said, '*We are going to play* Follow my Leader', but it was the first and last time I played that after I found out what we were going to do – we were going to get our flu jabs. We did get a chocolate biscuit.

Mr Green

There's a little bit more about Trueloves that I can squeeze out, about a certain character that used to come to the school. His name was Mr Green. I think he was a tramp, a lonely old tramp, who used to come to visit us. He walked for miles to come to visit us. He wore a grey flannel coat and a beret. We used to say if we saw him coming, '*Oh, here is Mr Green again*'. The teachers would make him a cup of tea and he would come and speak to us, but he was a bit of a nuisance, he was. We used to go riding and one time after I had broken my arm there was a knock at the window and it was Mr Green, who held his arm like it was broken like mine, making fun of me and I burst into tears. The teacher

My portrait of Mr Green

gave me a cuddle and I think the headmaster told him to go away. My brother and I told my mum and dad about this Mr Green.

One day we were mucking around with him and playing with him and we tried to lock him in the shed but the teachers stopped us. We were only kids.

A very strange thing happened. One day we were walking down the road by the hospital where my mum used to work, and a man was walking towards us and both my brother and me said, '*It's Mr Green!*' And she said, '*It can't be the same man*'. But it turned out to be the same man who came to visit the old people on my mum's ward. We don't know how he got from our school to the hospital. He probably just liked to be with people. We don't know what happened to him, but after a while he just stopped coming. All I hope is that no one was nasty to him. There's a lot more I could say about Mr Green but it would probably take up the whole book.

My mum's hospital ward

Sometimes I would go on the wards with my mum, I did, and the sister, Sister Herbert her name was, allowed my mum to bring me with her. I remember helping Sister Herbert give the tablets to the patients. Some of the old ladies were nice but some were a bit scary. They used to come after me. You know what it's like when you get old: you forget things.

In the hospital there was this man who used to work on the railways. I was talking to him one day and he said that he lost both his legs, he had. I said to lose one leg was sad, but to lose two legs was careless. One of the nurses ran to tell my mum what I had said. My mum came up quickly to apologise but the man just laughed and said I was right; he was careless. My poor mum, the things I used to say and what she had to get me out of!

Nightmares

Another memory I have of that age when I was at Trueloves: I had to have just three days off school because the day before I was due to go back to school after a weekend, we were watching the news on the television. There was a siege at the Iranian Embassy in London. They wanted to get rid of the Shah of Persia, I think, and I was a young boy watching it on the television. My mum wanted me to go to bed but I was too fascinated watching it all. All I remember is the SAS going into the embassy and a big explosion. I think I had a bad night that night, terrible nightmares about it. My mum and dad talked about it and agreed there was no way I could go back to school. I just had to stay at home for a while to get over it. Even now I don't know if I could go to Iran because of what I saw on the television and all I heard about that man, Ayatollah Khomeini. I don't understand it all. Even now if I hear his name and all that is going on in Iran, it gives me shivers down my back. If I see his picture I can't look at it. When I was younger, I used to think that he was standing outside my window when it was dark. I felt a bit scared. I would make sure all the curtains were drawn. Even now in my flat I like all the curtains to be drawn when it is dark. It's not so bad now though.

Let's try and find something nice now!

CHAPTER 4

MY THIRD SCHOOL: THOMAS DELARUE, 1983

Trueloves sadly had to close, it did, so we had to look for a new school. We visited a few schools and we found a nice one called Thomas Delarue School in Tunbridge, Kent. It was a Spastic Society School, which is now known as Scope.

Philip and I and a friend of ours from our old school called James joined the school on the same day. Philip went to a dormitory for older boys. James and I were in the same dormitory for younger boys. The leader of the house, the lady in charge of the dormitory, her name was Hattie. She was a very lovely lady, she was, but she didn't stand no messing around either!

Mum and dad left us and we had to settle down. James was in one bed and I was in another. There were three or four other people in the dormitory with us. I was a bit upset, I was. And Hattie said, *'Why is Richard upset?'* and James said, *'Because it's his birthday'*, so she gave me a kiss goodnight, she did. I think I was 11.

We didn't know where to go or what to do the next day. But we had assembly, we did, and the headmaster, Mr Tomlinson, welcomed all the new children to the school. Then we met our teachers. I remember that she was quite strict the teacher that I had, but she wasn't too bad. I remember the name of the class. It was 2B.

After the first term James, who had been with me from the age of eight, moved to a different class, he did, where he would do his GCSEs. I was more into doing artwork and sport and all that.

Thomas Delarue was twinned with a school in Germany. One year they would come to our school, and one year we would go to their school for a week. It was all done in draws – as in, they pulled your name out of a hat, they did, and if you were lucky you got to go. I was lucky, and so was my brother, and we got to go to the school in Germany. James and my friend Abbas and some care staff all went. There were about 20 of us. I can't remember too much about the visit but I know we went to meet the mayor of the village where the school was. We went to the Munich Beer Festival, we did. We sent a card home from the Beer Festival and my mum said, '*I thought the trip was educational!*'

A good swimmer

The school could see that I was a good swimmer, and the PE teacher said to me that I could go a long way in swimming, I could, if I put a lot of effort into it. So myself and Abbas (he was from Iran I think, but he was born in England; he was a deaf boy, he was), we were good at swimming, we were, so they got us in the swimming pool to compete in competitions. We had to get up at 6am, we did! There was three of us, there was, another boy as well. And the care staff, a member of the staff would be there when we were swimming. We had to swim from six to seven, or maybe seven to eight o'clock in the morning, but I know it was early! We would go away to compete in swimming meetings, we did. We did weight training as well, we did. I also had horse riding lessons at Thomas Delarue's. And some other boys competed in other things in the school, and at least six people in the school got places in the Paralympics in Seoul. This was in 1988. We were so excited, we were. The headmaster held a party at school for them before they went. While they were competing in the Olympics in Seoul, the headmaster kept telling us the news of how they were doing. Some students got medals I think, but I can't remember very well.

My stroke was backstroke. The way the PE teacher got me to go fast was to wind me up by saying my girlfriend was seeing someone else, she was, only joking to get me fired up. The best I ever got to in swimming was competing in the Nationals at Stoke Mandeville, and I just got beaten by a Scottish lady with one arm, but I got disqualified, I did. It wasn't my fault though. The organisers of the competition got our ages wrong. They put us in the wrong age group, I think. I worked so hard to get to the top, I did. The school and the PE teacher especially was annoyed that the organisers got our ages wrong – me and Abbas. The thing was, I had just been given a place up at the Derwen College up in Shropshire and I didn't really have enough time at the school to re-enter. As my mum puts it, she had her suitcase already packed to go to Seoul for the Paralympics. But I did get a medal for the relay race, I did.

I remember my dad coming to watch me. I remember my mum always saying to me, '*Don't look at us. Just keep your eyes on the swimming*'. But when I won my big race medal at Stoke Mandeville it was my granddad's 80th birthday party at home and I rang him up, I did, to sing him, '*Happy Birthday*', and to say sorry that I wasn't there, but he said I gave him the best birthday present ever by winning the medal in the swimming.

I must also add that I think that my mum wrote to my next school, the Derwen, to say that I was a good swimmer and could they find somewhere for me to keep it up and to say that I was having some golf lessons and could I keep that up. Nothing happened.

My art picture

My painting of a church

While I was at Delarue, also I did an art picture, I did, and it got entered into a competition and it won or came second, and the Queen came to have a look at the picture. I wasn't there. There were two pictures; one is an original and the other is a copy. One I kept and the other got exhibited all round the world. It got shown at the Royal Festival Hall in London. I think my poor brother got taken so many times to have a look at it, either by my mum and dad or by the school.

The school thought that I might be able to do a GCSE in art but I didn't do it. So I guess I wasn't very good at English or maths or writing things, but I was good at swimming and art. I left the school with my swimming medals and my artwork. It doesn't sound too bad for someone whose parents were told he wouldn't be able to do anything!

Leaving the school

I don't really remember leaving the school, what happened, but at the last assembly the headmaster said, *'Richard is leaving and he will be sadly missed'*. Philip had left the year before. The head said, *'We had two Bulls at the school and now it is the end of an era!'*

First of all, I said goodbye to James and I remember saying goodbye to a lot of my friends there but James especially as we knew each other from the age of eight to 17. Sadly we have lost touch but I knew that would probably happen.

A few years later, I just happened to be on the Tube in London with my mum, and we bumped into the headmaster of the school, Mr Tomlinson, who I hadn't seen for five or six years. I don't know if he recognised me or I recognised him but we got talking. He asked me how I was doing and I said I wasn't doing too bad. He said to me to see if I could try to get an NVQ, to try to get a qualification, because I think things were changing for people with learning disabilities. And then he got off the Tube, he did, and he went his way and we went our way, and I haven't seen him since. It would be hard to tell him now that I have an NVQ as sadly he died.

CHAPTER 5

PHILIP AND I GO OUR SEPARATE WAYS

This is the chapter in the book where I talk about my brother. Philip and I went our separate ways. It is as if we were on the same train and that we got to the train station and that the carriages split in half, they did. He went his way and I went my way.

Philip's way

Trueloves had reopened as a 16+ unit, so Philip decided that he would like to go back to the school. So he moved back into a house in Trueloves. But I just knew I couldn't go back there. I just had too many memories of when we were little boys there and what it was like. And I also think you should always move forward, never looking too much back. But my brother had some happy times there, I know that, so he went back. He became friends with two other men there. The three of them moved into a very nice bungalow, they did. And I must admit I did think a little bit, *'Well this looks nice'*. Maybe I was thinking I would have liked something similar. But I think the time had come for us both to live our own lives and to try to grow into men and to get our own independence. We are always in touch with each other and we care for each other, but he has his own life, now in L'Arche Ipswich, and I have my life, now in London.

My way

After the Delarue school I went to the Derwen College up in Shropshire. When we went for a visit to look at the college my mum decided, because my gran used to live up in Wolverhampton in the Midlands, she asked her if she would like to come with us and see the college, then she could see some relations. Granny thought that would be a good idea because she could see where I would be going, because she did take an interest in what I was up to. I remember that she planned a nice route for my dad to take to drive up there. My granny was trying to be helpful. She showed my dad the map. The only thing she had counted was that it was a straight route, but she was taking us on the railway line. We were going through fields. My dad said, '*We can't go on this route. It's a railway line!*' We all laughed about it. So we all drove off up to Shropshire.

I can't remember if we stopped at the B&B first or if we went straight to the college. I do remember that when we got to the college, my granny sat in the car, she did, while my dad and my mum and me went with some other families and their loved ones to have a look around the college with a lady called Mrs Edward. She knew Mrs Jean Kendall, the lady in charge of Derwen College, I think. What I heard was that you didn't want to get on the wrong side of Mrs Kendall! Thank goodness I never had that experience!

We had a good look around the college. And then after that we went to the café and we had a nice cup of tea and some cakes. Mrs Edward asked me and my mum and dad what I thought of the college. Then I said that my granny was in the car so Mrs Edward said, '*Let's get her out of the car and give her a cup of tea*'. So she came with me and we got her out of the car and she had a cup of tea. She had a good nose around, she did. I think she liked what she saw.

CHAPTER 6

DERWEN COLLEGE, 1988-2006

Derwen College buildings

I remember my first day at the college. I think I was 17, about 1988. All the new boys started one day, and all the new girls started the next day. Mrs Kendall met us. She and her husband, Mr Kendall, were the heads of the college. Mrs Kendall introduced us to the house mother who was going to look after us while we were at the college. She was a very sweet lady. She looked after all the new boys who had just arrived.

We all said goodbye to our mums and dads in the café and this is when I met Mrs Lyn Kendall, who was married to David Kendall. He was the son of senior Mr and Mrs Kendall. The senior Mr and Mrs Kendall were very well respected and liked and you knew where you stood with them! I was only there two years when the junior Mr David Kendall took over as head of the college. So you can say that the senior Mr and Mrs Kendall were like the King and Queen there, and the junior Mr and Mrs Kendall were like the Prince and Princess of Wales.

I just have to tell a little bit of the college history here, as I remember it.[1] It was founded in 1900 by Dame Agnes Hunt for 'crippled' children. Derwen Training College was founded in 1927, for disabled young people to learn a trade. On one side there was the orthopaedic hospital, and then there was the college on the other side, and one time they were linked together, they were. It was used for soldiers during the Second World War who had injuries and needed to be rehabilitated. It's amazing how it still keeps going, with all the cuts and changes in social care and all the challenges they had to go through, it's still a college for people with learning disabilities, over a hundred years after they started.

So, in the first term we had an afternoon when we went out with the junior Mrs Kendall and another lady. We went for a cup of tea. It might just have been the once now thinking about it, so we could get to know Oswestry, the nearest town. I think it was just to give us a little bit of independence so we could get to know the area and they could get to know us.

We were all given a counsellor, someone we could go and talk to about things. They would help you if you had any problems. I had a counsellor. She was just for a term or so then someone else took over. They used to see you once a term, just to see how you were and how things were going. If you wanted to talk to them you could make an appointment to go and see them.

Garden or kitchen?

In my first term we did one week in each department, just to see how we would get on. Mr Hogg was in charge of the boys and Mrs Roberts had the girls. We used to do woodwork with Mr Hogg. We would go to a different department in the college just for the morning to see how we got on there. I remember the garden department, the catering department and the sewing department. I decided to be sick that

---

[1] You can read more about the history on the website: www.derwen.ac.uk/about-derwen/derwen-timeline/

week of the sewing, and so I skived off, I did, but I think they caught on. The one department that I didn't go to because they didn't think I would be very good in it was the office department.

At the end of the term, Mr Hogg would talk to the head of the departments we went to and a few other people and they would ask us which department we liked. I had a long talk with senior Mrs Kendall (the Queen, though I wouldn't call her that in front of her face, I might get into trouble!). I said that I liked the catering department and the garden side, I did. I liked working with food and there was a good crowd in the garden and I thought I could be quite happy there.

Mrs Kendall said, *'Well, let's look at it like this, Richard, the gardens are nice to work in when it is nice and sunny, but when it's wet you get wet, and it's not very nice'*. She said that in the kitchen you would be dry all year round. So I thought about it and decided to go to the kitchens, because I don't like getting wet anyway. So after my first term with Mr Hogg, it was decided that I would work in the kitchens.

In my first week in the catering department, I remember one incident when I thought, *'What have I come to?!'* Some of the students from the college came from tough backgrounds. We were all standing in a line ready to start working in the afternoon. Two of the older students were having an affair, they were, and I think they had just had a row and it was a bit steamy in the kitchen, and I don't mean just from the food! Before the tutors – the teachers or the tutors or whatever you like to call them – came back from their dinner break, the girl got quite annoyed and said, *'I am not talking to you!'* The tutors came into the kitchen and one of them said, *'Who wants to help me do some cakes?'* and I said quite quickly, *'I'll come and help you!'* just to get out of the firing line!

On my second term we still had to go to Mr Hogg for one afternoon a week, so I was still a new boy. I just have to tell you a bit about Mr Hogg, what kind of character he was. He could be very nice and very kind and took a great interest in how you were getting on at the college, but if you did something wrong, like I remember I made a tractor and an aeroplane in woodwork, if you did it wrong or not how he liked it, he threw it on the floor and said, *'Go and start again!'* I remember one lad who was in my group who was a bit terrified of him. He went to work with the girls. But I think that at the end of the day he was just trying to see how much pressure we could cope with.

The lady in the coffee shop

The lady in charge of the coffee shop was a bit prim and proper. She was quite strict, she was, but she did have some good points. My mum and dad said to me that my mum would have to go into hospital to have some treatment, an operation I think. I can't remember if they told me what it was about, why she had to go into hospital. But, as I know now, she had gone into hospital for bowel cancer so she had to have an operation, she did. I remember I was working in the coffee shop and the telephone rang. The lady who was in charge working in the coffee shop that day answered the phone, she did. She said to me, 'Richard', she said, 'you have to go to the medical centre. There's a telephone call from your mum there is, yes'. So I ran down from the coffee shop to the medical centre. I think I would definitely have got a gold medal that day for running! I sat in the office at the medical centre. I picked the phone up. And it was my mum on the phone. She'd had an operation in the hospital, she had. Then she explained to me all that had happened and that she was okay now, she was.

A few days later, my granddad had to go into hospital for the same thing, I think. He got himself looked into after my mum had been in hospital and my poor mum had a bit of a relapse, she did. She had to go back into hospital, she did. I just remember breaking down in tears in the coffee shop because I had two members of my family in hospital, I did, at the same time. The lady in charge of the coffee shop was very kind to me and they all looked after me, they did.

CHAPTER 7

A TIN OF PEACHES

I have to tell you about an incident that happened at the Derwen. This is my legacy at the Derwen, what I'm remembered for!

On a Thursday afternoon in the kitchen we went into groups, we did, with an instructor. We did projects, we did. We made things. This particular project was called *Cold Sweets Project* as we were going to make cold sweets for the students for tea. The group I was in, there was myself and about five others, including a girl who will be very important in this story. She would come to haunt me for all my years in the Derwen. We'll call her Tracy.

We were busy doing rice pudding and we were putting peaches on top of the pudding to make it look nice. The instructor was in charge of the project group, but Tracy was also in charge – unofficially! I was busy doing what I was told to do and Tracy was in one of her wind-up moods. She was really winding me up this afternoon. She was giving her orders out and telling me what to do. I felt cross that she was being bossy. I was putting things in the fridge to cool down, and I said to one of the other girls who was in our group, *'She's really going to have it now'*, I said.

So I opened a tin of peaches, not a small one, but a big catering tin of peaches. The peaches were in syrup, they were. I just got the whole lot and threw it over her head, I did. Everyone in the kitchen was sliding over because of the syrup on the floor and poor Tracy was standing there with syrup all over her head, bits of peaches coming down over her face.

I thought I might get into trouble. So I just ran out of the kitchen, I did. I just wanted to hide, I did. I wanted to get out of the way. I was a little bit annoyed and upset with her; in fact, I was very annoyed. So I went to the medical centre and told the head nurse I wanted to see my counsellor NOW, I did. That was what I was like then. I needed to talk to her THEN. I told Mrs Rogers, the counsellor, all what had happened. She said, *'Well!'* I don't think she knew whether to be cross or to laugh.

One of the teaching staff who was involved with the project came over to the medical centre to see if I was okay, because I was very angry and upset, I was. What I believe is that the chef in the kitchen at the time knew what Tracy was like and said to her, '*You must have been asking for it*'.

There was me being calmed down in the medical centre with a nice cup of tea and Mrs Rogers sorting out what was going on, and all the people in the kitchen skating around on the slippery floor. Poor Tracy had to go off to her room to have a shower.

Because of who Tracy was, the top dog, she thought she was anyway, let's just say her boyfriend could have duffed me up, he could have grabbed hold of me. So Mrs Rogers talked to the nurse in charge that day and they thought it would be best for me if I was to have my tea in the medical centre that night, but after I calmed myself down and got myself together I said, '*No, I'm going to have my tea in the canteen*'. I think that evening I put the Derwen on red alert; everyone wondering what would come next. When I walked in, everyone came up to me and said, '*Well done!*' and gave me a round of applause, even her boyfriend I think. I think from that day, Tracy had a new respect for me, she did. She knew not to mess with me, she did.

Then the next day I did go to the kitchen and the chef was standing there, and he looked at me and I looked at him, and he said, '*Richard, at the end of the day, that was a really bad thing that you did*' – he was trying to keep a straight face – '*but you have got to look at it that it could have been a pan of hot water. It could have been a lot more serious than it was*'. And I avoided all the week the heads of the college, I did, because I was too scared of getting into trouble. But I think that deep down they did want to tell me off, but firstly they knew that she was probably asking for trouble, and secondly, they found it hard to keep a straight face.

And that's the end of the peaches story. I think Tracy had a bit of a bad background. She used to call me names. I think that we will leave it there. I don't think she was really loved when she was younger.

CHAPTER 8

AN OPERATION

When I was a trainee in the coffee shop I was in my flat. I had to go to the medical centre as I was getting pains in my stomach and I wasn't feeling very well. Nurse Roberts was on duty. She gave me a tablet, she did, and told me to go to bed. The pain did ease off a bit, but later on that night it came back again and I had to ring the buzzer in my room. The nurse who was sleeping in that night came over to my flat and gave me another tablet, she did. I think it was a bit stronger. She said she would put me down to see the doctor in the morning.

So then next morning I wasn't feeling too bad, but I wasn't feeling good either, so I went to the medical centre and the head nurse was there (she was a nice nurse, she was, but she could be a bit fiery). *'Oh'*, she said, *'You are down to see the doctor'*, but she could see I wasn't feeling too good. It was my day off from work so I didn't have to go into work that day. So someone came to my flat and told me the doctor was there. So I went back to see him. He gave me a once-over, he did, looking at my chest, doing what doctors do. He said that he thought it was my appendix and he would put me down for an appointment in the hospital. He said it wasn't much to worry about.

I went to the café and sat with my friends, I did. I don't think I ate all my dinner but I ate some of it, I did. After I finished my lunch, I did what they had told me to do and went for a rest on my bed. I was only lying on my bed for an hour or so, then let's just say that the pain was really getting quite bad and I started to be not well, let's just put it like that, and I had to press my buzzer again. This time a nice member of the care staff came over to my flat and she said, *'Don't worry Richard'*.

But this time I was in a lot of pain, I was. She rushed me in a wheel-chair with a bucket in my hands down to the medical centre. I was really quite weak at that time. They called the doctor to come back again in an emergency and he took one look at me, he did, because I was quite red in the face then, and I was quite sweaty, I was. They were giving me things to cool the fever down. So he phoned for the ambulance, he did. Mr Thomas said to my mum and dad on the tele-phone that I looked as red as a snooker ball, I did!

The first ambulance broke down, it did. They got quite worried at the college, they did, wondering where the ambulance was. It was about three hours later, it was a long time, the night staff were coming on, and a different ambulance arrived. By this time I didn't know what was going on. I was quite red in the face and very hot. One ambulance man and one ambulance woman came in. I think the ambulance people were having a love affair because of the way they were talking. The lady ambulance nurse wore a short skirt so couldn't bend over to lift the stretcher into the ambulance. The male ambulance driver and one of the nurses, who was quite little, and a member of the care staff, who was quite little as well, carried the stretcher into the ambulance. By this time there was a crowd of people outside the medical centre seeing what was going on because it was a big thing when an ambulance turned up at the college. Everyone would come out to see what was going on.

So in the end it was a clapped-out old ambulance that took me, and I ended up going to the Shrewsbury Hospital, I did. I had to go to the hospital on my own. The nurse said there was no one to go with me but she felt bad about that. The ambulance drivers just put me on the bed in the hospital and left me, they did. Then the doctors and nurses on the ward came and did their stuff, what they had to do. They were very kind to me and put me at my ease, they did.

I was operated on at 10.30 that night, I was. I remember saying to the nurse that I wanted my mum, I did, and my mum saying to the hospital it would take them five hours to get there. They were quite worried at home, they were. But it just so happened that we had a relation who worked at the hospital. My mum and dad got in contact with her. I was really quite poorly so I don't remember much but I think Sally, that was her name, came down to see how I was. All I remember was that I was quite thirsty and I said that I could drink the ocean and the Atlantic all at once, I could. Me mum would have come down straight away if she could but as me dad said quite rightly, *'He wouldn't be in any fit state to see us, he wouldn't'.* So they came to see me a few days later, they did.

The day after I had my appendix out, when I felt even worse than I felt before I had my appendix out, the lady in charge of the trainees came from the Derwen with John, a good friend of mine at the college, and Jane, my girlfriend at the time. They brought loads of cards for me, they did, from people. They read them to me, they did. They stayed for just about an hour and I think that Jane was a bit upset to see me lying there in bed with tubes coming out of me. She was a bit worried about me, she was. She gave me a kiss goodbye, she did. I think they got back to the Derwen and reported I was alive, but not kicking.

Me mum and dad came down a few days later to see me in hospital. The nurse said, 'We need to get you up today, Richard. We need to get you looking all nice and well for your parents'. I spent about a week in hospital, I did. Then I came back to the Derwen and spent a few days in the medical centre, but they said I wasn't allowed to lift anything and I wasn't allowed to go back to work for at least six weeks, I think.

When I moved back into my flat after the medical centre I took it very easy. I took my meals in the dining room with the students so I guess I was treated like royalty for a bit. John came in from work, he did. He gave me a box. They had made me some nice cakes in the coffee shop, they did. Then my mum came down to stop for a few days in a B&B. She came and nursed me for a few days, she did. We went up to the coffee shop with me holding her arm because I was still a little bit weak. The senior Mr and Mrs Kendall were sitting in there and straight away they came up to me and my mum and said, 'It is good to have our old Richard back again'. That made me feel really welcome and pleased.

CHAPTER 9

THE VISIT OF THE DUCHESS OF KENT

Everybody knew that I am a big royalist. Rumours were starting to spread around the college that the Duchess of Kent, who is the patron of the college, had been invited to come to visit the college and to open the new medical centre. So I asked the lady in charge of the coffee shop if I could have the day off work to see the Duchess of Kent. I was very lucky – I did get the day off work. The lady in charge of the coffee shop, who was like Hyacinth Bucket, she was very prim and proper and liked things to be done properly, said to me that she was very lucky as she had been invited to meet the Duchess in the social centre and to have something to eat with all the other members of staff at the college.

I just felt pleased that I was going to see her. It was a private visit. It was just for the college so it was very low key, it was. But she was going to go to the orthopaedic hospital next door and then come to us in the afternoon. I remember on the morning of the visit there were lots of police and sniffer dogs early in the morning walking up and down the college, checking it all out. But I was very lucky because Mr Kendall knew that I liked the royal family and he gave me the schedule, he did, with the timings of when she would be coming. I remember that I think it was about 10 o'clock in the morning or maybe a bit later, I saw a big red helicopter fly over and land at the orthopaedic hospital. I went running up to the café where all the higher hierarchy as I call them were having their morning cup of tea. I think I nearly collapsed with excitement because I had seen the helicopter. I remember two police officers, who were also having their cup of tea in the cafeteria, said to me, *'Oh, if you had come here straight away we could have told you that, because we heard it on our walkie talkies'*. They were joking.

It was sometime in the afternoon after she had done her visit in the hospital that everybody started to stand outside and a crowd started to gather. Everybody from the college was standing outside. Mr and

Mrs Kendall and all the governors, in fact all the heads of the college, were dressed up very smart, they were. I think some important people from Oswestry were there. One of the students of the college got a bunch of flowers to give to her when she arrived.

Two police motorbikes came into the grounds of the college with their lights flashing. A big black posh Daimler, or whatever you like to call it, came into the grounds. All I know is that it had lots of windows so we could see her. We all cheered and we went, '*Wheyaa!*' that she had come to the college. She got out of the car and came over to talk to us, she did. I got to say, '*Hi! How are you?*' Then she walked into the medical centre, and Mr Kendall and senior Mr Kendall did a bit of unveiling for the naming of the medical centre. She unveiled a plaque, she did. Then I think she looked around in the medical centre, then she came out and walked into the social centre and I believe had a cup of tea, met lots of people, had a bite to eat, then hopped back into her car and went back to the hospital to get back into her helicopter to fly back to London.

How I knew that she had a cup of tea and something to eat was because I was quizzing everyone as they came out of the social centre. Mr Kendall said to me that her lady in waiting said to him that she had to get back to London to get changed to go out to some posh evening somewhere. Sometimes she had three events to do in one day sometimes.

That was the day the royals came to the college!

CHAPTER 10

GIRLFRIENDS

I think it was in my first term that I met my first girlfriend at the college. She was in my year, she was; she came at the same time. We just slowly became good friends, we did. I'll call her Elizabeth. She was a lot more brainy and brighter than me. I think she only had a physical disability not a learning disability. It is funny; I can see her now as I talk about her. It's weird. I've got a picture of Elizabeth somewhere.

In our first term or our second term, I can't remember which, we were allowed to go into Oswestry on our own. The first time we had to go with a care worker. Elizabeth was standing one side of the road and I was standing the other at the bus stop. I wanted to go into Oswestry but wasn't sure of the buses, which direction it was into Oswestry, even if I was at the right bus stop. She said, '*Can I help you, can I?*' and I think I said, '*Yes, that would be very nice. Thank you*'. She helped me to get to Oswestry on the bus. Let's just say that was the start of a happy relationship. It ended later with a story involving me and a cupboard!!!

As our relationship grew, Elizabeth invited me to go and stay at her house for the weekend to meet her family. So I did. We got to her house. She was laughing at me, because she said her sisters were very nice, and they were, and her parents, but they had a great big dog, they did. We arrived at the house, and Elizabeth rang the doorbell so we could get in. Then there was a '*Woof! Woof! Woof!*' The dog, it's fair to say, pinned me down on the floor. He was a nice dog, he was; he just wanted to be friends. Elizabeth grabbed hold of the dog and said, '*Go into the bedroom, Richard*'. The dog just needed to calm down, it did. After the dog and me got to know each other we all had a good weekend.

Life had moved on. I had been working in the coffee shop for a year or so now. We used to have fancy dress discos, we did. I remember one disco Elizabeth and I dressed up as two cleaners. We had the uniform what the cleaners used to wear. I had a wig on my head, I did, and a towel tied up like an old washerwoman and a pretend fag in my mouth, I did, and a mop and bucket each, we did. I can't remember if we won;

I think we came second but we made everyone laugh, we did, coming in with our mop and bucket. The Kendalls were the judges, they were. Mrs Kendall was laughing saying, *'They haven't done a good job, those cleaners!'* having fun. I might have had lipstick on but I can't remember.

Me dressed as a cleaner at the
Derwen, 1991

I remember another event where I dressed up as a woman in the Christmas concert. Me and two other boys dressed up as three women and we came on stage and we sang, *'Sisters, there were never such devoted sisters...'* from the *White Christmas* movie.

Elizabeth did her three years at the college like I did. But she's very bright. She worked in the office at the college. She left. We said our goodbyes and our lives went in different directions. I knew she was going on to bigger and better things than I could ever do, like working in an office. We tried to keep it up. I stayed on in the college and worked in the coffee shop. But with time we just drifted apart. I do believe that Mrs Kendall told me that when she wrote to the college to see how things were, she always asked how I was. My mum and dad were very fond of her.

Girlfriend number two at the college was Jane. I knew Jane quite a while before we went out because we worked in the kitchens together. All I can say really about our relationship was that it was very hot and cold sometimes. But we had some good times, we did. We just found out that we were better friends than in a relationship, we were. We went on some nice holidays together.

When I had been working in the coffee shop for a year or so, Elizabeth came up for a visit, she did, to the college. I was a bit surprised to see her. I was now going out with Jane. I didn't know what to say to Elizabeth so I took the easy way out of it when she came into the coffee shop to see me. I saw her coming and hid in a cupboard!!!! I didn't want to hurt her but in the end I did pluck up enough courage to go and talk to her and I like to remember the incident because we parted friends.

CHAPTER 11

ENGAGED BUT NOT MARRIED

And now my third one. This relationship is about a girl I went out with that I'll call Sarah. I guess that Sarah and I really got to know each other because we got talking to each other on train journeys coming back to London to meet our families from college. I remember my dad once putting me on a train at Euston. He bought some doughnuts and he gave me one, he did, and he saw Sarah sitting next to me and he said, '*Perhaps this young lady would like a doughnut?*'

I would say she was out of my league, she was. I wasn't good enough for her. I remember that she had just broken her arm. She had just split up from her boyfriend, she had. So I thought, '*Here's my chance!*' I went to visit her in the medical centre. She was sitting there. I said to her, '*Would you like to go out with me, Sarah, would you?*' She said, '*I'll think about it*', she said. And to my amazement, she thought about it and said, '*Yes*'.

Our relationship grew. I went on a family holiday with her and her mum and dad. It has to be said that Sarah had a few more disabilities than I had. But she knew her own mind and she was very independent.

I went on holiday with her and her family to France. And I knew that after the holiday my dad would come and pick me up from the airport and she would go back to where she lived, and I remember sitting at the airport with her as we waited for our plane back to England, and I didn't want to say goodbye to her. I said that to her, I just didn't want to say goodbye.

Engaged

I think we talked about it there. We talked about getting engaged, we did. I remember we did get engaged, we did. I think it is fair to say some members of our families were really pleased we got engaged. But I think others had doubts about it.

Everything was all planned at the Derwen. They found two flats for us to live in as a couple. But the deal was that we would have to get married first. But as anyone who has been to the Derwen knows, there are some nice bungalows at the Derwen there are, but I think because of our benefits system, we wouldn't be able to have a bungalow because it would change our benefits. So it was better for us to have two flats. We started to live together for a few months and the wedding had been planned, it had for September, but I slowly began to think that the pressure of it all was getting too much for us both. We had to give away a lot of our things to make room for things in our flat, we did. It wasn't at all easy.

And then Sarah went to visit her parents, she did, so I was in the flat on my own. I think I phoned my mum up to wish her happy holiday because she was just about to go away on holiday with friends of hers, and she said she had received a letter from Sarah's dad and mum saying that they wouldn't let Sarah and I live the way we wanted to live and they wanted a lot of say in the way we were going to live our marriage. I guess what I am trying to say is that Sarah's dad wanted to keep his rights to have a say in Sarah's life and I wouldn't have any say really. And I wasn't even meant to know about this letter and nor was Sarah meant to know, but my mum thought it was right that I should know. So I thought long and hard about it. I remember I had a really long bath, I did. While Sarah was away, she was meant to come back the next day from home with her mum and dad; I just went to the lady in charge of the trainees. And I said to her, '*I just can't do this*', I said, '*I'm going to have to call the engagement off*'.

Calling off the engagement

Anyway, my mum had gone away on holiday with her friends. The lady in charge of trainees phoned my dad up to tell him what I was going to do. She said to me, '*When Sarah comes back to the flat tonight*', she said, '*get the college to give me a ring, and I will come to the flat to be there with you. I also have to be there for Sarah*', she said. They came back to the flat, they did. I saw them coming and I phoned the college. My heart started to beat, beat, beat, it did.

Sarah came bouncing into the flat like she used to do. We were practising sometimes in the flat her writing *Keagan-Bull*. We were so happy. But they walked into the flat, they did. Her dad could see that something wasn't right. He said, '*Are you alright Richard?*' I said, '*Yes, I am. You'll just have to wait*'.

The lady in charge of trainees got there so quick, she did. I was on one side of the table with her, and Sarah was on the other side with her mum and dad. She said, '*I am here for Richard, but I am also here for Sarah*'. I said that I was going to call off the engagement. But I couldn't really explain to Sarah why with her parents there. She just threw the engagement ring at me and ran into her bedroom, banging the door. It was an evening at the college that I never want to go through again.

Everyone tried to talk to Sarah, they did. Then the lady in charge of the trainees said, '*You can't stay here in the flat tonight*', she said. So I went and slept in the medical centre, I did. I just remember I phoned my dad up and he came down to see me, he did.

But then I found out that, let's just say that some nasty letters were going round from Sarah's family to my mum and dad's friends who were going to come to the wedding, saying things like: my mum and dad institutionalised my brother and I; they sent us away to school. They said some really horrible things about my mum and dad, they did, which I feel really bad about. Even some people phoned my dad up because they were upset about what was being said about my mum and dad, about my mother especially.

Sarah was telling everyone that I was not good at some things. Let's just say that I just felt raped inside, I did. These are strong words and I am sorry about it. I don't think that Sarah even knew about the letters or anything that was going on afterwards, but for the next two years at the Derwen, she wouldn't speak to me or say anything to me. I think the icing on the cake came when her ex-boyfriend said to me, '*Sarah and I are back on now, we are*'. She used to call me every time she saw me going to church, '*Bible basher!*' She used to call me names.

Leaving Derwen

After our relationship ended, I tried to stay at the college. I really gave it a go but after two years I just knew that I couldn't stay any longer. So I packed my bags. I remember my dad came to help me pack up all my belongings. We walked down to the coffee shop for some dinner and Sarah just walked the opposite way, she did. She saw my dad and just couldn't look at him. But I had a good send-off party at the college.

My last day of working in the coffee shop at the Derwen, I took my uniform off and put my other clothes on. When I said goodbye to everyone, I had tears in my eyes and I think they all had tears in their eyes. We were like a family in the coffee shop, we were. Happy memories! I always remember the leaving party I had in Kelly's Bar. People were queuing up to come. We had a meal, we did. Lots of people were there.

I had some very happy times at the Derwen, going ice-skating, falling flat on my face ice-skating and being picked up, going on very many happy trips to Alton Towers and Blackpool. On my last day, some of the cleaners all came to say goodbye to me. It was very hard after being there for so many years to say goodbye to some of the senior members of staff like Mrs Kendall, and all the staff. They were very kind. They always had time to listen to you if you wanted to have a talk. I was very glad to have been at the college and I'm always proud to talk about the Derwen to people. When I go to meetings and that, I'm always very proud to say I went to the Derwen College in Shropshire, I did. I spent 17 very happy years there, I did, and made many good friends.

I learnt about life there, about being independent, being always on time for work, what the world is like, to always dress smart and all that.

So then I left the college, and do I have any regrets? I have some regrets, I do, in things I have just said, and there are friends that I miss there now. But I made the best move because I'm living a lot more independent life now, I am.

And so let's just say, 'Goodbye to the Derwen and hello to L'Arche! Out with the old, and in with the new!'

PART II

FINDING A VOICE

CHAPTER 12

MY FIRST ENCOUNTER WITH L'ARCHE, 2006

My mum first heard about L'Arche on *Woman's Hour*. She heard how it had been started by Jean Vanier, an ex-naval officer who had invited two men with mental disabilities to leave the institutions where they were living and to come and share his life.[1] Now there are communities all over the world – people with learning disabilities sharing their lives with 'normal' people.[2]

I guess my first encounter with L'Arche Lambeth was when I came for a visit.[3] We visited L'Arche in Kent and in West Norwood, London. I came with my mum and dad and brother. I think we all looked like the Mafia, we did, walking up to West Norwood. It was Louise who we were coming to meet. I remember the first thing she said to us after she welcomed us was, *'Who would like a cup of tea or coffee?'* And it just felt right the way she made me feel comfortable and at ease. She did say that they were just starting to have people living independently in their own flats and that perhaps it would be good to have me live in my own flat and be supported by the community.

So Louise gave us a guided tour round the workshops where I met the leader of the weaving workshop and other people who worked there, like Brian. Brian was telling me he was doing his weaving and he was telling me he liked going to Blackpool on the rollercoasters and he could take me. And I thought, *'You might think it mate but you won't get me on a rollercoaster!'*

After our visit we went home, we did. I liked it in the L'Arche community in London. It was about six months later that I came to live here. It was 3 July 2006. Because my learning disability is not as bad as some, I am able to live in my own flat, but as part of the community.

---

[1] This was written before I heard about the allegations against Jean Vanier – see Chapter 35.

[2] For more information about L'Arche, see: www.larche.org.uk

[3] Now called L'Arche London.

My mum was trying to tell me to be not too upset if people from college don't keep in touch with me because people move on and start anew.

I remember that when I first came I was going to stop in the Elmstone, one of the homes in the community, for four weeks just to let my feet settle down on the ground. We knocked at the Elmstone door, we did, and Flavio, who was house leader at the time, opened the door with an apron on and a spoon in his hand. He was busy cooking, he was. I remember that evening my mum and my brother left me because they went back home. First of all, the community leader came to say hello to me and to welcome me to the community. And then we ate some supper in the Elmstone and I got to know the people who lived there.

And in the evening Jacek came to see me. He was the man who was going to become my assistant and help me find a flat. He stayed and talked with me for half an hour. We're still friends and keep in touch.

Louise said she wouldn't be here for my first night as she was away doing something so she wouldn't be able to welcome me. The next evening Louise was sitting outside in the courtyard of the Elmstone. She came up and welcomed me saying, *'It is good to see you!'*

Me with Louise Heatley at a '70's themed party at L'Arche London

This is where I need to introduce Hazel. She is my friend who helped me to write this book. She is like one of the dames in my life story. If this book gets made into a film, Dame Judi Dench could play her. Hazel has been part of the furniture in L'Arche for many years. She often arranges the celebrations and liturgies, with a lot of coloured cloths and jugs.

I think that I was only in the community for a week when Flavio said that Hazel had asked the Elmstone to help her with one of her liturgies. Flavio said to me, *'All of the Elmstone will be helping Hazel with her liturgy. Do you want to help?'* And I thought, *'Well, I don't know who this lady is, but in for a penny in for a pound!'* So I said yes I would. There was me, Brian who I had met in the weaving workshop who was also a big man, and Hazel, in this little red car and with loads of cloths, driving off somewhere.

Hazel said, *'It's very nice to meet you'.* They were trying to tell me all about the community, they were, as we were driving along the road in this little red car. Hazel was saying they liked community life but they find it difficult when assistants come and leave after one year. When we got to the church where we were going, we all sat on the floor on cloths, we did, and Hazel made a great speech which I can't remember now but it was to do with the Bible reading. There was a woman vicar there, there was. It was fun I remember.

If I want to explain what L'Arche is like, I'd say there is always room at the table. I can go to one of the community houses for dinner, or to the workshops to have a chat. L'Arche isn't a nine-to-five job for the assistants, and they aren't superior. We often gather together for birthdays to tell stories and listen to each other. We like to celebrate.

CHAPTER 13

MY OWN FLAT

At some point I had a meeting with Louise and Jacek. The day after I arrived in the Elmstone, Louise was saying, *'Right, we've got to make a plan, we have'*. She said that we've got funding for four weeks for me in the Elmstone, she said. Jacek couldn't support me every day because he had his job in Mencap to do, so he supported me on Mondays, Wednesdays and Fridays, and Louise supported me on the other days.

I remember me and Jacek walking up and down West Norwood High Street going to estate agents finding out about flats. But we also did some other interesting things. He took me out on the buses so I could learn some of the bus routes. He took me to some of the restaurants so I could find out where to go and eat, and so did Louise when she was supporting me.

Some of the estate agents were not very nice to me. When they heard about benefits and all that I was on, they weren't all that interested. I was getting quite worried in my head because I had moved from the college and we just had four weeks to find what we were looking for or I might have had to go back home and end up coming in by train each day to find a flat.

The Derwen very kindly left my place open for six weeks at the college, just in case it did all fall flat. I remember that Jacek and I went to a letting agency in West Norwood and Jacek said, *'Let me do the talking and see what happens'*. So the man from the agency took Jacek and me to this flat down a nice road in West Norwood. I just looked at it and everything felt right about the flat, it did. He said, *'Leave it with me for a few days. I'll talk to the landlord about things'*. And then after a few days he came back to us and said that the landlord is quite happy for me to move into this flat. *'As long as he's got his money at the end of the month that's all that matters to him'*. So in August 2006 I moved into my flat.

Before I moved into my flat Louise asked me if I wanted Jacek to continue supporting me if he would agree to. She said that if I didn't they

Me in my flat in 2022 (1)

Me in my flat in 2022 (2)

DON'T PUT US AWAY

could have interviews to find someone to support me but I said I was happy for Jacek to continue supporting me. Jacek very kindly agreed to support me for the five hours' support I had each week.

I remember my first day in my flat. It was quite an exciting day, it was. Jacek very kindly came to meet me at the L'Arche house where I was staying. He could only come in the morning. He had some things to do in the afternoon. He helped me move in the morning. The community leader was very kind and said that I could have some things from the house just to start me off.

The first thing that Jacek and I had to do was to go to the letting agency to give them a cheque for the first month's rent. The woman who worked there read out to me the tenancy agreement: the things I can do and the things what I can't do. We got to the flat, Jacek and I did. The first thing what arrived was my nice double bed what I bought. Jacek and I had a cup of tea with the kettle what we bought and two mugs and we had a drink to celebrate my moving into my new flat. We sat on the bed, I think.

My brother and my dad, who I spoke to earlier in the day on the telephone, were coming down in a van with my stuff. They got a bit lost, they did. They did make it in the end, they did, and put my stuff in my flat for me. My brother was going to stay for one night in my flat if I wanted him to, so I wasn't on my own, but we decided, or I decided, that I would be okay. My dad said that '*Your mum would like to come and see you in your flat*'. So my mum came to see me the first or second weekend I was in my flat just to see how I was and how I was getting on.

I just remember her saying to me just before she left that she was very proud of me for living in my own flat on my own.

Niagara Falls in my kitchen

The nearest community house to my flat was the Sycamore. Corinne was then in charge of the Sycamore. She said if I needed anything in my flat just to call the Sycamore, she said.

My first weekend in my flat I turned the sink on in the kitchen at the weekend and there was a leak and water started to come out of the sink and it was like Niagara Falls in my flat! My first weekend and I had a flood in the kitchen and I thought, '*Crikey! What's going on here?*' I think it was a Sunday and the letting agency was closed and I didn't know who to ask for help so I just phoned the Sycamore. I didn't know the people in the Sycamore well and Corinne was away on holiday for that week, but someone came and helped me call the plumber. I felt a bit stressed and a bit anxious. It was all new territory to me and I didn't know how to deal with it. The plumber came and fixed it all for me. I had to pay him, I did. I told the letting agency about the flood and they gave me back the money what I paid the plumber.

The man who lived in the flat next door to me, who I didn't know very well at the time, he just knocked on my door to say they had a bit of a flood in their flat coming from the leak in my flat. I thought, '*Oh crikey! My first weekend in my flat and I've already upset the neighbours I have!*' But he wasn't too annoyed about it. He was okay.

I realised in my first few weeks in my flat I had really made it in the big wide world, I had. I was pleased that I made friends with Corinne and Hazel and Louise and Jacek and everyone in the Elmstone. And I was pleased that I had found a nice church to go to who also made me feel welcome.

CHAPTER 14

SHOPPING ON MY OWN

One of the first things that I did on my own, I was going to go on a cruise with my family and I wanted to buy something nice to go on the cruise with, so I took myself off into Brixton, I did. I had no one supporting me or helping me to do this. All I wanted was just something to go on the cruise with and I came back from shopping with a white jacket, white trousers (it's really shiny white!), black shoes and a dinner shirt. I did try to explain to the man in the shop that I didn't want the trousers but I don't know if buying the whole lot was a good thing I did or whether he talked me into it and whether I look a right banana in my white suit. It doesn't come out very often, I can tell you! I think I showed it to Louise, Flavio and to Jacek. I think they said, '*Oh dear Lord, Richard, yes, it looks very nice!*' They were very polite about it.

My cruise suit

I did actually wear it for L'Arche Lambeth's 30th birthday party. The party was in the gardens of Lambeth Palace and the Archbishop of Canterbury came. I wore the whole lot, I did. I wore a black hat as well. It was a trilby I bought at Greenbelt.

CHAPTER 15

OFFICE VOLUNTEERING

I had a conversation with Louise in my flat. I said to her that I wanted to do some work in the community or something. So she said, '*I'll have a word with Hugh, the community leader, about what he thinks might be best that you can do*'. I think that he had a word with Kate in the office. Thanks to Kate, she allowed me to go and help her on a Friday to do the information sheet for the community. So that's why I went to the office on Fridays. I sometimes also answered the telephone as well. I made sure everyone got the information right for the week hopefully, with the help of Kate, and later Tim. I really enjoyed my time going to the office helping them. It helped me feel part of the community a bit more. And I sometimes went to have lunch in the weaving workshop. I've worked there now for about 13 years, yes. It was all very nice.

Sometimes when we were writing the information sheet, Kate and Tim liked the information in by Thursday at least so it can all be typed up ready for Friday. But it didn't always work like that, it didn't, like when people called up and said '*I've got some information for you*', just as we were about to print it.

And it was just nice going into the office because I got to see my friends and people in the community who passed by the office.

We used to eat lunch with the people in the workshops. Like Brian when he was alive and working in the weaving workshop. Brian loved beetroot. He would try and kiss one of the people with learning disabilities with beetroot all round his mouth for a joke so that was quite fun, it was. She would shout, '*No Brian!*' It all used to be fun, it did. He would chase her round the table, and she would shout, '*No, Brian, no!*' We all laughed, we did.

When a sad thing happened

I remember I came to work in the office one Friday and Kate and I were just starting to do what we were going to do. One of the assistants who works in the community was going to have a meeting with Jacek. Maybe about five or ten minutes later Jacek went running out the office, he did, and then everything all started to go a bit weird, it did. Then Kate had some telephone calls, she did, and then she went off, she did. Then about an hour later or so, Kate came back to the office and she told me that Anthony had died (one of the people living in L'Arche). That's why Jacek and everyone was running around. Everyone was being busy sorting things out and supporting the people in Anthony's house. I felt really quite sad about it because I had become a friend of Anthony, I had, and was on his circle of support. He died on his birthday. Kate gave me a cuddle, she did, then.

CHAPTER 16

DURHAM REGIONAL GATHERING

I was quite new to the community in L'Arche, only about a year, when I went to the L'Arche Durham Regional Gathering. A Regional Gathering is like a jamboree, when lots of people from each L'Arche community in the UK come together to celebrate being part of a big organisation. It happens every few years.

Me and Hazel as MCs for L'Arche UK's Regional Gathering, Durham, 2007

Me and Corinne at L'Arche UK's Regional Gathering, Durham, 2007 (1)

Me and Corinne at L'Arche UK's Regional Gathering, Durham, 2007 (2)

When L'Arche Lambeth arrived at the meeting in Durham, the two people who were in charge of the accommodation for our group had to rearrange everything so people were near the people they were going to support. You could say the first night L'Arche Lambeth played musical beds! Or musical rooms as we were changing rooms! After a long journey to get there the last thing we wanted to do was to do that. One of the ladies in our group wanted to sleep on the floor.

For some reason, I don't know why now, someone asked if I would help Hazel on the stage to welcome everyone each morning and evening, which I think she regrets now! People didn't really know much about me then. Hazel said to me the first day when we were on the stage, it is going to be quite quick, we are leading people into prayer and we need to be quite serious. Somehow when I got hold of the microphone, I turned it into a comedy show. Each time I made up stories about Hazel and other people in L'Arche Lambeth, saying things like: *'Did anyone see Hazel abseiling down Durham Cathedral with a bottle in her hand last night?!'* She looked quite horrified when I said that! Everyone burst into laughter and clapped while Hazel was trying to keep it all serious. We enjoyed being together.

L'Arche certainly do know who I am now... once seen, never forgotten!

It was good at Durham to get to know people from your own community in a different way and to get to know people from other communities. I got to learn a lot in those few days about the people in my community, and I think the same could be said about them: they got to know a lot about me. It was nice for everyone to come together and to be L'Arche and to have fun. L'Arche does know how to party!

A memory from Corinne:[1] *I remember the event in Durham was one of his first gigs on stage. He was a natural with the microphone and told everyone a story of how we made our getaway from drug dealers we picked up outside Paris!*

[1] Corinne McDonald, leader of L'Arche Lambeth at the time.

CHAPTER 17

NATIONAL SPEAKING GROUP

The National Speaking Group[1] was set up in L'Arche UK for people with learning disabilities in the communities in the UK to be able to have a voice to be heard so people can take part in big decisions in L'Arche UK and in their local communities. I became the first chair of the National Speaking Group in 2007. It started a year after I came to L'Arche in 2006. We had a meeting in L'Arche London with the community leader, who was Corinne at the time. She got us all together, all the people with learning disabilities in the community, and we were all sitting down and she said to us that L'Arche had thought of this new idea to have a National Speaking Group for people with learning disabilities in L'Arche, to be able to take part in things what were happening in L'Arche. She said that we needed to have a discussion and a vote to decide who would become our representative on the committee. We had a vote, we did, and I got elected, I did, to represent L'Arche London at the Speaking Group. I felt quite excited but quite nervous as well.

I was also a little bit nervous about going to this big meeting on my own in Crewe, I must say, and not really knowing anybody. I remember sitting on the train on my own not knowing where I was going and what I would be doing, wishing I had someone with me just to be with me for this first meeting. I got a taxi from Crewe train station. I just showed him the details of where I had to go and all that, and he took me to the place where the meeting was being held – I can't pronounce it – Wistaston Hall. As soon as I arrived there, a lady called Kathy Mac, she looked after me, she did. And there was another lady there who also made sure I was okay. They were from L'Arche Liverpool. Then all different people started to come from around the UK.

It was at this meeting that we had to set the ground rules about how the meeting was going to be working. So the first evening was

---

[1] Now known as *National Speaking Council*.

just getting to know each other. I think we all introduced ourselves, we did. We were all sitting like a proper board meeting with tables. Kathy Mac said that we've got to elect some people to do some jobs in the meeting. And that we had to elect a secretary, a treasurer – no, there's no money involved because L'Arche doesn't have any! We had to elect a secretary and some people to do some other roles and we had to elect someone to be chair of the committee, Kathy Mac said. So Angie from L'Arche Ipswich became the first secretary, she did, and sadly Angie has died now, she has. And then we had to elect a chair. Lots of people wanted to become chair, they did. So we had to go out the room, the ones that wanted to become chair. There were three of us, then it came down to two of us, and then the third time we came back into the room, it was me and a lady from Bognor. Kathy Mac said to me, '*Well done Richard! You've become the first chair of the National Speaking Group!*' So she said, '*It's over to you now to get the agendas done*'. And for some reason, I do remember this, we all sang a song, 'Old MacDonald had a farm'. I don't remember if she thought it was funny or not, because her name was MacDonald.

And then we got down to some serious stuff, we did. We had to arrange for a meeting in London with Kathy Mac, Angie and me and the other supporter to plan the next meeting, our first proper meeting of the National Speaking Group. But I do remember coming back from the first National Speaking Group meeting on the train feeling quite pleased with myself, I must say. I phoned my mum and dad and said I'd become the first chair of the National Speaking Group and then I phoned Hazel, I did. I think the power went to my head a bit, it did. I said to her, I now wanted a plane, I did, to get to the meetings. I said I had become the President, I did. I think I promoted myself a bit! I also phoned Corinne, the community leader, and told her. But I also remember that evening I treated myself. I went to Café Rouge I did. I felt quite pleased with myself, I did. Not only did I travel all the way up to Crewe on my own but I'd also just been elected to do a big job for L'Arche.

So I remember being all proud going to our first planning meeting in London a few weeks later at the Friends' House in London by Euston. Angie was going to be supported by an assistant for the first meeting and I was going to be met at Euston by Kathy Mac and the other supporter, I was. We all met in the Friends' House and had some nice sandwiches, we did. Kathy Mac said the words what I will never forget; she said, '*Have you been told about going to India yet, have you? And going to talk to the Federation about the National Speaking Group?*' I thought '*Blimey, they put you in the deep water already without swimming in the shallow end first, in other words trying to get to know things!*' I said, '*Okay then*'.

So there it all began!

CHAPTER 18

INTERNATIONAL FEDERATION ASSEMBLY IN KOLKATA, INDIA

Going to India

I remember having a conversation with Hazel, just vaguely, and she said, she just mentioned the word, she said, *'Have you ever thought about going to India, Richard?'* and I said, *'Definitely not! I don't think so!'*

A few months later after having spoken with Hazel, I got an invitation from the two International Leaders for L'Arche, inviting me to go to India! This was in 2008. I talked with Louise, who was my support worker at the time, and I wasn't really quite sure whether I could do this trip or not. We wrote an email to Hazel (because she was in charge of organising the meeting and knew what things were like in India), explaining exactly the conditions that wouldn't make me comfortable in India, like not having a proper bed to sleep in, having too many people in one room, eating rice three times a day and not having someone to support me. Hazel very kindly worked her magic, she did, and she emailed us back and said she had managed to arrange for me to have a room with the L'Arche UK National Leader and a man from one of the Indian communities who was very nice. And she said there would be someone to support me.

So I agreed to go. It was interesting to go to a different country. I had heard about India but had never been and it was good to see what India was really like.

Corinne, who was then community leader here in L'Arche Lambeth, said she was going to come to India with me she was. She would support me. The L'Arche UK National Leader, John Sargent, who I didn't know that well, very kindly said that he would help to support me if there was anything I needed help with. He came to a meeting in Lambeth and made time to have a meeting with Corinne and me to talk about the things L'Arche International wanted me to do in India. Let's just say it wasn't going to be a holiday!

So Corinne and I arrived at Heathrow Airport. Hazel at this time was already out in Kolkata. We showed our boarding tickets to the air staff for the BA flight and I got upgraded to first class, I did, on the plane, but Corinne didn't. I could spread out and sit comfortably. That was really quite good, that was! And when I turned round I could see Corinne through the gap reading her newspaper in ordinary class. We arrived in Kolkata after about 13 hours I think on the plane. And half the people (well actually only two) from L'Arche UK who were on the plane with us were dying for a cigarette!

First few days in India

Corinne and I were very lucky in that we were stopping in a very nice hotel for a few days before the meeting started. When we arrived in our posh hotel, it felt very nice but also felt not right in a way because we were in a nice hotel and we could see the real India outside, cars racing up and down, cows walking along the road. But it was good because we did need to get ourselves acclimatised to the conditions in India. My one memory of going from the airport in Kolkata to our hotel was seeing a man walking up the road with a stick in his hand dressed like Gandhi with just a white cloth wrapped around and not very dressed. It made me feel a bit sad and it felt a bit odd and strange, it did, being in a foreign country. It made me feel how lucky I was to have a nice warm bed and a nice flat.

But I must say that everyone in India was very nice and very kind to us. I remember that Corinne and I, after we'd had a rest, went for a walk. And then we came back to the hotel to have something to eat in the restaurant and guess who was there? One of the National Leaders, a few other ladies and – Hazel! We all gave each other such a big hug and cuddle I think all the staff in the hotel thought we were completely bonkers! Everyone was jealous because Corinne and I had a nice swimming pool in the hotel to swim in and they didn't!

One day, Corinne and I were going to visit the temple of the goddess Kali in Kolkata and they had just had a big rainstorm, they had, and Corinne said to me we had to take our sandals off because we couldn't walk in our sandals because it was a holy place. I slipped on something, I did, and fell flat on my back, I did. I was in a lot of pain, I was. I just wanted Corinne to come and help me. But these three big Indian men picked me up, they did, sat me and Corinne onto a rickshaw and this poor Indian man was running through the streets of Kolkata, pulling us, me in pain. It was very hot. The sun was beating down on us and he got us to a taxi and the taxi driver and the rickshaw driver put me in the taxi with Corinne and I was in a lot of pain and couldn't walk. I just wanted to get to the hotel.

And then we got back to the hotel. The hotel staff got a wheelchair and put me in a wheelchair, they did, and I went back to my bedroom and they put me on the bed, they did, these Indian men. I was still in lots of pain by this time. They brought some ice up to put on my leg. I think they wanted me to go to the hospital in India but Corinne said, '*I think we'll try and see what we can do before we go to the hospital*'. They gave me some tablets in the hotel and some spray for my leg and with the help of Corinne she got me walking a little bit up and down on it.

We knew we had a day and a half before the meeting started to get it all working properly. I remember we had our evening meal brought to the bedroom for us, room service. They put a flower, a rose, on the tray, they did. That was very sweet of them.

The meeting place: where we stayed

We got to the meeting after going up and down the road a few times in the taxi because he didn't know where he was going. After we said goodbye to our nice hotel with the nice staff who looked after us and the nice food and the nice evening meals we had, we got to where the meeting was and I went to where my bedroom was and Corinne went to where her bedroom was. She was sleeping in a room with 50 other women and I was sleeping in a bedroom with just two other people, John (the UK National Leader) and Peter, a man with learning disabilities from Chennai who was a friend of Hazel's. I felt quite grand really when I thought about Corinne lying there with 50 other women and a few spiders, I think. I had my own shower, I did. I've never had so many showers in one day because it was so hot, it was!

In my bedroom there was no air conditioning like in the hotel. There was a big fan what went whishing round in the sky in the room. And John said to me, '*How was your stay in India so far?*' and I told him about our nice hotel that we stopped in and about being upgraded on the plane. He told me about flying into Kolkata and how he had some beans for breakfast and a boiled egg and a bunk bed. It wasn't as nice as I had. He had stopped in a local hostel. I think it was the YMCA. All he had for a shower was a bucket, I think.

But we were very lucky in our bedroom because we had a shower room, just for myself, John and Peter. John very kindly helped me to put my mosquito net up, he did. We didn't have one of those in the hotel, we didn't, because we had air conditioning there. We had to climb into our mosquito nets. It was difficult. I think the net fell down a few times. We had lots of laughs, we did. I think I was downgraded a bit from my nice hotel, and John Sargent was upgraded a bit from the YMCA.

I remember one evening I went to have a shower in the bathroom. I was getting myself all ready to go to bed when I put my hand on the sink, which wasn't very tight anyway, and the whole lot just fell off the wall and smashed on the floor, it did!

Peter and John jumped out of bed so fast, faster than ever in their lives, I think. I said, '*I've broken the sink I have!*' John said, '*We know! But are you okay?*' John came running into the bathroom, he did, and I think he stopped the water from coming out. I was a bit shocked, I was, and a bit amused. John remembers I had my silk pyjamas on, I did.

Before I came to India, Hazel said to me, '*I'll be very busy so I won't be able to see much of you, but if you need me, just say "Stop" and if I can help I will*'. So the next day I did see Hazel running past, and I said, '*Stop! I've broken the sink in my bedroom! It's come off the wall*'. She looked a bit surprised, and said, '*Oh dear!*' and tried to keep a straight face. And I think she had a word with someone and they mended it quite quickly.

My memories of India are, first of all, that we were welcomed with garlands of flowers and we were blessed with red powder on our heads. One day we listened to Gandhi's grandson who spoke to us. We had to get into that venue a couple of hours before he arrived. We walked there, we did, in pairs. Everyone carried a yellow umbrella, they did, because it was so hot. We walked in silence following our founder,

Jean Vanier, and a man dressed as Gandhi. Well some of us walked, and some of us went by minibus, meaning me, because I had hurt my leg at the beginning of the trip. Gandhi's grandson looked like Gandhi, he did.

The meeting in India

Richard with Wendy Lywood, the Anglican priest from Daybreak, at the meeting in Kolkata, both in Indian clothes

I was asked to go to the meeting to give a talk about the National Speaking Group in the UK and to spread the word so other countries could do the same, because our National Speaking Group was the first in the world. So I am the first chair of a National Speaking Group in the whole of L'Arche. There were 500 people listening to me speak, including the founder of L'Arche, Jean Vanier. People came up afterwards and asked John and me questions, how we did it, how it really worked. They were interested to do something similar back in their own countries.

I also remember that Jean Vanier stood on the stage with the two international leaders and went on his knees and asked forgiveness, he did. A lot of people said, '*Why is he asking forgiveness? He has started this wonderful community at the end of the day*'. But as we all found out later, he was asking forgiveness for something else.[1]

Then I remember we had elephants, not real elephants, but they were really big; they needed several people to carry them. We walked outside, we did, following the elephants. There was a band playing and Jean Vanier was sitting in a silver chariot drawn by horses with Peter sitting with him, the new friend I shared a room with in India. Peter has a learning disability and he is one of the elders of the communities in India, he is. We were celebrating Jean Vanier because it was the last international meeting that he was going to come to. And I don't think anyone really knew what was going to happen but we all soon found out. We ended up throwing coloured powder at each other, we did, and we ended up with col-oured powder everywhere, we did. People might have wanted to lock us up because they might have thought we're all barmy, but actually it's part of some Indian festival, it is.

On the last evening, we walked out carrying lights on a leaf, and we went to a large pond and laid these leaves with candles on down on the water. It was nighttime and it looked beautiful with the lights flickering on the pond in the night sky. I thought, '*What a nice way for us to finish the meeting*'.

Every day people from L'Arche International filmed me to give a bit of a talk that day about what we had done that day, and the talks we had listened to. They did the same with a Frenchman. Just the two of us. I felt quite important as I was reporting back to the UK and other English-speaking countries.

I remember the last time I said on the video, '*I am looking forward to the pilot saying, "It's raining back in England, and it's cold"*'. And I was looking forward to a nice bacon buttie, I was. But on the flight coming back, before we came in to land at Heathrow we got our breakfast, and it was curry!!! And I felt, '*This is just what I didn't want!!!*'

When I think about that meeting, I learnt a different way of life, a different culture, just how poor some parts of the world are, and how rich we are in this country and how much we take for granted, and how warm and welcoming people were in India.

[1] See Chapter 35.

CHAPTER 19

VISIT TO AUSCHWITZ

This piece of writing was written after my visit to Poland in August 2008 for my summer holidays. The vicar at the church that I go to asked us if anyone wanted to write anything about their summer holidays for the church magazine. Hazel asked me if I wanted to write anything and I said yes, and she very kindly wrote what I dictated. I think she was just expecting me to write about going to the beach, having a few ice creams and watching seagulls landing on the sea or something, but instead I talked about my trip to Auschwitz. She was quite surprised and quite moved with what I said.

I went to Poland with two other people with learning disabilities and three assistants from our community for our summer holidays. I had heard about Auschwitz and really wanted to visit. Jacek was visiting his family in Poland at the time and joined me for the visit to Auschwitz. It was just me, one of the assistants and Jacek who went. We decided it wouldn't be appropriate for the two other people with learning disabilities who went on the holiday.

I've used the article in talks what I've given. I went to St Ethelburga's in London with Hazel and read it there.[1] She was telling peace stories and she thought it would be nice if I came and read my piece about Auschwitz. I think I read it at Greenbelt as well. People were quite sad and moved by what I read out. My dad has copyrighted it for me. I put it on Facebook a few years ago and a lady in Belgium from L'Arche International asked me if she could use it. She sent me a message afterwards:

Dear Richard,

Last Wednesday I went with an international group of long term assistants, to Auschwitz. In preparation of that day, I explained what happened to people with disabilities in that period of our history. I also

---

[1] St Ethelburga's is a centre for reconciliation and peace in the City of London.

read your text. It was very silent in the room. People were deeply touched. Thanks for sharing your reflections. I will let you know if I would like to use it in other formations.

Christine Bruggeman.

I'm pleased that people are hearing what I am talking about and hopefully learning from my words.

My article for the church magazine about my summer holidays and my trip to Auschwitz

I found it very moving. Just walking around and looking at some of the things there. What shocked me the most was that everyone had labels pinned to their prison uniforms and I asked Jacek, my friend, what label I would have had. I don't think I would have been here today, nor none of my friends. I think that if I were there they might have decided to do some tests on me in their so-called 'hospital room'.

And I was just so pleased that there was me from England, Jacek from Poland and the female assistant who was from Germany all standing there – together, and I just ask that we try and learn from our mistakes and that this never happens again.

It made me quite angry it did, and I wanted to kick something I did, but with a lady being there I felt I shouldn't do that. I feel quite angry inside now I do – about the way they were treated like cattle – like they weren't worth anything. I can see now why people who lived through that, when they see those uniforms, they feel sad and angry.

I think in life we should try and understand each other and work things out and never want war – just be happy with what we've got. It doesn't matter if you're black or white, if you can speak or if you can't speak – it's what you can give that counts.

CHAPTER 20

MY ADVENTURES: AUSTRIA, ITALY AND ATLANTA

I'm calling this chapter 'My adventures' because I did a lot of travelling around Europe and the world for L'Arche. I was representing the National Speaking Group for L'Arche UK, because I was the chair. My mum says L'Arche is my travel agent!

Austria

In Austria we were going to a meeting of all the leaders of L'Arche from around the world, and some people with learning disabilities from different countries. The people with learning disabilities had our own group: François from Brussels, Anne-Leticia from France and Maricia from Slovenia. Maricia was very funny and learnt to speak some English. We settled down to our work: talking about what we need, what our fears are and what we can give. Some of the things people said were very powerful and true to what they feel. Later, when we rejoined the other group, we agreed many of the same things.

On Day Two we talked about *Commitment & Belonging*, including the things that make it difficult and the things that we like. While we were talking we used pictures and drawings to explain what we wanted to say. For some of the time together, the two International Leaders joined us. They were pleased to see us working so hard and were surprised by some of the things we said, as was the main group. I am afraid to say that I kept falling asleep during the afternoon.

That's what I did in Austria. And then I was tired! I felt quite important and very proud that my views and voice were being listened to. We all had our picture taken together, like the UN after an important meeting! Then we got our plane to head home.

Me at an international meeting

Me with Stephan Posner, then the National Leader of L'Arche France, at an international meeting

Me speaking at an international meeting

Italy

I went to some meetings in Bologna, Italy – the land of spaghetti bolognese. But we did not get any – I am still waiting for my spaghetti bolognese! But pasta is better than the rice I got in India! The meeting was for all the L'Arche Coordinators from around the world. There were 60 people there.

In the talking group I took part in, there were two ladies from France with learning disabilities, and a gentleman from Belgium with learning disabilities, and there was a nice lady with learning disabilities from Slovenia who had her own translator. Four people who were at the meeting in November in Paris (which I couldn't go to because I was on a cruise going to Egypt with my family! It was a good way of missing a meeting!) couldn't come because L'Arche International couldn't afford it. Some people were upset these people couldn't come and I said, *'Perhaps if they saved money by having fewer coordinators come, they could have come'*. Someone very kindly translated from French to English for me and from English to French.

After our meetings in the day we went back to the assembly to tell them what we had talked about in our little group of people with learning disabilities. I got on the microphone on the second day and I asked all these important coordinators to put their hands up to say whether when they got back to their own communities after the meetings, they would spend some time with people with learning disabilities in their own communities and only about five or six people put their hands up and I thought, *'What have I done?!'* I thought I had asked an embarrassing question but the International Leaders said I had done a very good job. I heard afterwards that everyone remembered my question!

The three subjects we were asked to discuss were assistants in the communities, and how to talk about L'Arche to more people outside our communities, and the third subject was money but we only managed to talk about two subjects.

People in our group found it difficult to understand what assistants in their own communities were saying because some assistants don't really know how to speak the proper language of the country. One of the ladies from France said that she went out for a day trip once with two assistants from another country and they were speaking in their own language and she had to ask them if they were speaking about her because she couldn't understand and thought they were speaking about her. I said that in my community, assistants are told to speak English in front of the people with learning disabilities.

I said about spreading the word about L'Arche, that we go to Greenbelt in this country and lead celebrations there.[1] I said the people there find it very moving at the Washing of the Feet when someone in a wheelchair washes the feet of someone else without disabilities.

We talked about many other things and finished the week off by going for a nice ice cream and a nice walk.

Our group did the prayers on the last night. Everyone had a candle to light and had to lay it down on the floor. We got everyone up and dancing. We took the reading from the one in the morning about Jesus being judged and all that. I said, *'Look at the body. Look at the eyes and look at the tears of joy and sadness. Look at the heart and feel the love for you. We are all one body. We are all equal'.* I said that in the prayers.

I think the meetings were good and it was good they included people with learning disabilities but they do need to speak in an easier way and with more pictures for us to be able to understand what's going on.

I had quite an adventure coming home because stupid British Airways went on strike. I got home but only just – we had five minutes to catch our plane!

---

[1] See Chapter 30

Atlanta

I got invited by L'Arche UK to go to the L'Arche International Federation meeting in Atlanta. Tim, who works in the office in our L'Arche community, we both went. When we arrived in Atlanta, Tim and I went to stay with Tina (who organised the meeting) and her partner Anna. At Anna's house we watched what was going on in England: the pageant on the Thames, what was going on for the Queen's Jubilee. I was a bit gutted, I was, to be missing all that, all the royal stuff that was going on in England. I gave Anna a tea towel to do with the Queen's Jubilee as a thank you gift. I think she's still got it. I'm not sure. Maybe I'll have to go to Atlanta to find out.

The meeting began. We all went to look at different projects around Atlanta, we did. I went to a school for young children under eight years old, or a bit younger than that. We watched them. I think it was a school for children with autism, with behavioural problems. We watched them in the classroom, we did, and then we went outside and had a water fight with them. I remember these children squirting me with lots of water, yes. But we weren't allowed to take any pictures there, well, not of the children, no. I think there might have been some official photos taken. Tim had gone to a homeless centre to make food for the homeless.

I remember that Tina said to me, '*Oh Richard, would you help us tomorrow to interview the President of the college where Martin Luther King used to go to?*' So I said, '*Okay then, yes*'. Tim and I had started to do the pilgrimage walk to the church where Martin Luther King preached. Then halfway round the walk Hazel grabbed me saying, '*Oh they're waiting for you at the church*'. And somewhere along the pilgrimage I lost Tim, I did, but Tim did know I was going to give a talk. So then we got to the church. I got a bit upset because I lost Tim, I did, and I thought we were going to meet at the church. I think I was with John Sargent, I was (the L'Arche UK leader who shared my room in India); I don't think I was on my own. I think that John could see that I was starting to get a bit tired because they were asking me to do a lot of things. Oh yes, CNN was coming that evening and they wanted me to talk to them. I remember John turning round saying, '*Do you mind Richard? I'm going to take charge now. After this it will be enough for Richard*'.

The gospel music in the church was beautiful, it was, as people entered the church after doing the pilgrimage walk. So I pulled myself

The L'Arche UK delegates to the International Federation Assembly in Atlanta, 2012: James Cuming, Chris Bemrose, Istvan Jabok, Me, Hugh Durant, Louise Carter, Tim Spargo-Mabbs

together, I did. Hazel stopped what she was doing. She could see that things were getting a bit too much for me, and she just sat with us. That helped me to feel less stressed.

So me and another man from L'Arche went on the stage and we interviewed a man whose name I've forgotten, who's very important: the President of the college where Martin Luther King went. I had the whole of L'Arche, 500 people, watching me in the church where Martin Luther King preached. I asked him, 'Did he think Barack Obama would become president for a second term, as they were having elections then?' I kept asking him the same question but he couldn't really answer it, but I kept pinning him down but I think he wasn't really allowed to answer such questions. I think the audience laughed. I felt very good, I did, giving that interview. It was quite a big thing to do, a privileged thing to do, to interview the President of the college which Martin Luther King went to.

Thinking back, it was a bit of a roller coaster: one minute you're up, one minute you're down, one minute you're upside down on your head, you are, and then you just pull yourself back together again, and you just get on with it. I just went up on the stage and I just did it and I shone, I just came to life and just shone and just did it. I felt that was quite an achievement, it was, and I felt quite proud of myself and lots of people were coming up and saying, 'Well done Richard'. And that made me feel good, really good.

CHAPTER 21

PILGRIMAGE IN CANADA

Hazel said to me that she had been invited to go to Canada and they were asking if I wanted to go with her. I agreed and said, '*Yes, I would come to Canada with you Hazel, yes*'. Why we went to Canada is that L'Arche Western Canada were having a regional gathering. We were being asked to lead a pilgrimage out there for them. While we were out in Canada, we did three different pilgrimage walks in the three different areas we visited. One member from each of the communities, founder members, started the pilgrimage walk off in each area by carrying the cross. At the end of each walk, we all sat down in groups, we did, and washed the feet of everyone in our small group. It was really quite beautiful, it was. It was also nice to go to Canada, for Hazel as well as for me, to meet again old friends we had met in India. This was in 2011.

After we got to Heathrow Airport, we booked ourselves on the flight and all that. We had quite a lot of time to spare, we did. So we went into the perfume store, we did. And tried on all the sprays, we did. So I don't know what we smelt like when we got on the plane! They must have thought, '*Cor blimey, what do they smell like?!*' I asked everyone if I could be upgraded on the plane, saying I had just had my 40th birthday but they said no.[1]

When we arrived at Calgary, a lady from L'Arche Calgary met us at the airport. She took us to Pat's house, who we were going to stay with. He was the one who had invited us to go to Canada. Hazel said, '*I know where to go*', because the lady driving hadn't been there before but Hazel had. But when we got inside Pat's house Hazel said, '*I don't remember that wall being there!*' and I thought, '*Here we go! What mess has Hazel got us into here?!*' I thought, '*I've just had a long flight and here we are strangers in a foreign country in the wrong house!*' Hazel kept saying, '*I don't remember this*', and then a strange man walked in and I said, '*There's a strange man coming in who looks a bit worried*', and I thought, '*Oh, we're going to spend the night in the cells in Canada. We'll both be put in handcuffs because we are in the wrong house!*' But the man

[1] See Chapter 28.

Me and Hazel and leading a pilgrimage for L'Arche
Western Canada, 2011

turned out to be Pat after all. He said he had done some work on the house and altered the layout of the main room. So that explains what had happened.

I think that Pat was getting quite stressed about the work we were going to do in Canada, hoping it would all go to plan. After the barbecue we went to bed and slept and slept and slept. I had the posh room and Hazel had the library.

One day we went swimming in the mountains with some people from the community. I said to Hazel, '*I haven't got any trunks, I haven't*'. But they said you can get trunks to borrow there, you can. It was just nice swimming seeing the mountains all round and with the hot springs. It was just beautiful, being able to relax and I bought a T-shirt, I remember.

We went to church with them in the evening. The priest turned the sermon into question time, he did. It turned into a real heated discussion, it did. Then at the end when he went out down the aisle, he took his cassock off and threw it over his shoulder and walked down in his jeans!

The next day, Carmel from L'Arche Edmonton came and we went straight into work. Pat always laid the table nicely for breakfast. We had croissants and pastries. Hazel had her laptop on the table, Carmel had her laptop on the table, Pat had his laptop on the table and I helped them do some work. I helped Carmel prepare name badges for the pilgrimage. Hazel was busy preparing the liturgies for the meetings. Then I went to a community house and watched a film with them, I did. They were very nice to me and we ate popcorn and crisps and had a real proper film night.

One day, Carmel, Hazel, me and Pat went to meet some nice nuns at the top of a hill. I asked them to pray for Patrick, a man in our community who was dying.

The pilgrimages

At the first meeting in Calgary there were about 150 people there for the regional AGM; then there were about 500 people for the next few days. One day we all walked up the hill to the nuns. It was all arranged that we would get there and start to sing and they would come out and greet us. But we arrived too early and had to wait for them to finish their afternoon sleep. They were very elderly! But then they came out and blessed us and they gave us all some nice chocolate. We then quietly went back down the hill, well as quiet as L'Arche can be, which is not always quiet!

Then 'The Hazel and Richard and Carmel and Pat Road Show' moved on to Vancouver. We stayed with a nun who was very nice but quite strict. We did another pilgrimage walk there with the communities of Vancouver and Comox Valley. There were about 150 people.

Hazel and I acted out having a row. We enjoyed practising it! I was disagreeing with Hazel, saying, *'Oh you're driving me nuts, you are; I'm not going away with you again!'* and Hazel said, *'I'm not going away with you again!!!'* Then one of the ladies from one of the L'Arche communities stood up and came over and told Hazel off. She said to her, *'Breathe slowly!'* Then she told me off, she did. She slapped me on the bum, she did. I think she thought we were having a real argument! But we were going on to talk about the importance of forgiveness. That's what it was all about.

Ever since then Hazel and I keep having arguments and back in England L'Arche Lambeth don't know what to make of it! But we're just playing.

On our day off, two ladies from L'Arche Vancouver drove us up into the mountains and we met Sister Claire, who made us feel very welcome but the dogs who were there didn't make us feel welcome. They were barking. I think they were to keep away intruders and bears and that. We met some of the other sisters who were in the convent up there. We had afternoon tea with scones. Sr Claire took us out and we went for a bit of a walk. She showed us the new building which they were building where the nuns will live and where there will be guest apartments. It was very beautiful.

There were some trees which were like curtains opened up. When we walked between two of the trees Sr Claire said, *'This is the entrance to my cathedral!'* The view on the river on the other side was really really beautiful. We walked to the river to see if we could see some salmon spawning and Sr Claire said maybe we might see some black bears if there were salmon around. And Hazel said, *'Whoopity doo dah!'* but I thought, *'Yes, but not too close!!!'*

Hazel said, *'Oh we might see some eagles flying around!'* She wanted to see some eagles. But we didn't see any eagles, and sadly we didn't see any bears. We did see some salmon doing grown-up things, we did; they were making new salmon. But sadly, after they did that, they died. After that we went back but stopped at a large river and saw lots of seals swimming.

The whole pilgrimage was very reflective. It was very nice to meet the people in the Canadian communities and to be so welcomed. I think the Canadians enjoyed our visit and liked my English accent!

After our trip together I made jokes about it. I'd say, *'I'm still on the medication for it; I'm still taking the tablets after that trip with Hazel'.* And Hazel would say, *'I don't know if I'd go with you again!'* but we were both just joking. I would do it again, I would, tomorrow. Well maybe not tomorrow, but I would do it again. It was fun. I enjoyed it. It was hard work but it was good to get to meet other communities from around the world.

This is a photo of me and Kathy who I met when I was in Western Canada. On her trip to England we met up and I cooked a three-course meal for her and Hazel. I wore my Banff t-shirt. I'm holding a photograph of the community there that welcomed me.

CHAPTER 22

THE FIGHT TO KEEP MY FUNDING

It was about six or seven years after I joined L'Arche London. For the first six years of being part of L'Arche London, Shropshire funded my five hours a week support in my flat. It has to be explained that I am originally from Essex and when I went to the Derwen College in Shropshire, Essex funded me. And then, Shropshire took over and I was given these grandfather's rights it was called 'cos I had been at the college for a long time. That meant that Shropshire continued to fund me at the college. But when I decided to leave, Shropshire decided I would only get five hours a week support in my flat and that would be all. I remember that the lady who was in charge of my support and care at the Derwen explained to me that Shropshire had agreed to fund me for five hours a week in my flat. And she was quite strong but clear it would be only five hours' support a week. I wouldn't be allowed to work in the workshops in L'Arche London. There would be no funding for it.

Six years later I got a telephone call from Shropshire saying they would like to come and have a face-to-face meeting with me. I thought to myself, *'Oh this is going to be big. They've never come down to see me before'*. It made me a bit worried because they just phoned me up once a year to see how I was.

So the social worker came from Shropshire. It was a lady. My mum and dad came to the meeting. Jacek was at the meeting. And the social worker said, *'We think it is time after six years for Lambeth to take on your funding'*. I felt a bit uneasy about it and not very sure that I wanted this to happen. I felt uneasy because I have a mild learning disability and they might not decide that I need the funding. She said, *'Oh it will be okay. Lambeth will just take on the funding'*. But she did say just to be careful how I answered some questions.

So a few weeks later, a social worker came to see me from Lambeth. He seemed very nice, he did, at the start. There was me, Jacek and the social worker. And he was with me for a good couple of hours, he was.

And he asked me lots of questions, he did, and he was putting ticks by boxes and he was doing an assessment of me, he was. I didn't feel very happy about it. I was feeling uneasy about some of the questions he was asking me but it was his job. He was asking me questions about how I cope in the bathroom. If I need any help with personal stuff and all that. Washing in the morning and going to the toilet. And what help I need in the bedroom area. It all felt a bit personal. Then he asked what help I need paying bills and all that. Instead of saying the things what you can do, you really got to put the worst out. You got to not say the good things about yourself, but the bad bits. It doesn't make you feel easy. It makes you anxious inside.

After he finished he went away and it took a long time to hear back from him. I was quite anxious and wondering what was going on. And the social worker from Shropshire kept asking me, *'Have they got in touch with you?'*

And then I got the news I was worried about. Shropshire social services told me. They said Lambeth said I didn't reach the criteria of what they funded. So I said to the social worker on the phone, *'You said it would be alright, you did!'* and I just threw the phone on the floor, I did. And I came up to the community, to L'Arche, I did. I don't know where it all came from but I just threw some furniture around, I did. Let's just say I rearranged some furniture in the office, I did! I ended up on the floor in tears and Kate, who was working at the office at the time, could see that I was distressed, sitting on the floor upset and she just gently talked to me and two people who were working in the office were trying to put the furniture back in its place. I told Kate all about what had happened. And then the manager, Jacek, made lots of phone calls to find out what's going on.

So then the fight began to keep my support hours. I remember a few days later Jacek saying to me, *'I'm not really supposed to tell you this Richard, but I'm going to a meeting now in Lambeth about the incident what happened'.* And he said that there's going to be him there, the social worker from Shropshire and the social worker from Lambeth.

I don't think the social worker from Shropshire turned up. I had to go at some point to see the nurse. Just for an injection for a blood test, like the annual health check. And she just said, *'And how are you today, Richard?'* and I just burst into tears, I did. And she said, *'You'll have to tell me the whole story Richard; what's going on?'* So I said, *'I'm going to lose all my funding in my flat, I am'.* And she said, *'Let's forget about the blood test',* she said. They got me a cup of tea and some biscuits. And she said, *'I will have to talk to L'Arche',* she said, *'and I will have to talk to the social worker in Lambeth'.*

So she had a nice chat with Jacek in the community to find out what was going on. And then she phoned the social worker in Lambeth and told him off, she did, and said that Richard does need his support hours, he does. And after about an hour and a half later, or maybe a bit less (I was there for a long time), I came back to my flat feeling a bit more relaxed and there was a knock at my door. And it was the social worker from Lambeth. He made out that he had come to see someone else in Lambeth but he said he had just come to see how I was on his way to see this other person. He stayed with me for a good half hour or maybe even more. I think he may have had a cup of tea with me, yes. And he said could he just look at some paperwork in my flat. And he said, *'Richard, I am sorting it',* he said.

We also got an advocate to speak on my behalf. So with his help and with the nurse's help at the doctor's surgery, and the support of my mum and dad and the L'Arche community leader, I did get my support hours and in the end the social worker from Lambeth increased them from five to six hours. He put an extra hour on. He ended up from being not a nice social worker to being a nice social worker, not too nice but nice. At the end of the day, he just needed to try and save some money, he did.

And now I get my support paid for by Lambeth. I think it also helped that I was the co-chair of the Assembly for People with Learning Disabilities in Lambeth.[1] I'm quite well known, I am. The social worker did say at the end that I got the funding. He asked if I was happy with L'Arche supporting me. And I am happy with L'Arche.

And that's the end of that story.

[1] See Chapter 27.

PART III

BECOMING A CHAMPION

CHAPTER 23

PEOPLE FIRST AND THE FUNDING CUTS, 2007

I never thought after leaving the college in Shropshire that I would end up doing the things what I am doing now. When I came to L'Arche I didn't really have anything to do, I didn't. I did a few years at college, I did, in Lambeth. I did lots of courses, I did. It was good, it was, and it was a good way of me getting to know my way round Lambeth a bit. But I just woke up one morning and thought, *'This isn't really what I want to do with my life'*. I already spent 17 years of my life at college, I did.

Becoming co-chair of the Partnership Board

I went to a Partnership Board meeting in Brixton with my support worker, Louise. The Partnership Board is a voice for people with learning disabilities and their carers so they can say what they want to be going on and for the councillors to report back to them. Louise said, *'I think you might find this interesting, Richard'*. I had never been to a meeting before, definitely not one like that. As I found out, they had all the heads from Lambeth Social Services there and they had a co-chair, Gina, a lady with learning disabilities. She was very friendly. They had a co-chair from the council helping Gina chair the meeting. He was a man.

So the meeting started. I forget what they were talking about but I do remember I asked one question, I did, to the commissioners and the important people in the room. It was after the meeting that the lady who supported People First came up to me and said, *'You're new; I haven't seen you around here before'*. And Gina came up with her. *'Why don't you come to People First, one of the friendly meetings?'* And so I went to one of their meetings and got to meet everybody who goes to the friendly group. They were looking for a new rep to take over the job from the chair so they asked, did I want to go for an interview for that job as well? So I did. I got the job for one of the reps for people with learning disabilities to be on the Partnership Board. What it meant was we were going to have to go for meetings with Gina and her support worker.

After a year Gina stepped down as co-chair of the Partnership Board as she had had enough of it. So at the end of the day we were looking for a new member from the council to be co-chair. The other man with learning disabilities who was the other rep, he got another job working somewhere else, he did, and so it was left down to me, it was.

The council meeting about the cuts

Things were going to get a bit difficult with cuts and all that. The government said they needed to save more money. We had a new government in power then. I went to a meeting at the library in West Norwood, a council meeting about all the cuts that were going to be made in Lambeth. One of the councillors was there. I went to sit together with her because I knew her from meetings I had been going to. She said that Mencap had lost some of their funding for some of their activities that they do for people with learning disabilities.[1] She also said before the meeting started that they have had to take the funding away from People First. She was sorry to tell me that. So I thought, *'Oh great!'* I thought, *'I've become co-chair of the Partnership Board'*, and I thought, *'I've not had my first meeting and I've already been sacked, I have!'* I felt really bad but I didn't know what to say or do at that point.

But what's even worse, I phoned People First up on the Monday and spoke to the lady who used to help run People First. I thought they already knew about it but they hadn't heard that they had lost their jobs. I said to her I went to a meeting about the cuts and all that and got told by a councillor that People First had lost their funding and she said, *'What?!'* so in a way I told her she was out of a job. The manager of People First, who I think just heard the same day about what was going on, I think he was going to tell them the sad news.

They said to me, did I still want to chair the Partnership Board meeting? It was going to be quite an angry meeting, it was. I said, *'Yes, I would'*. They both said to me they wouldn't be able to support me in the meeting as they normally did because people were quite upset and annoyed that funding had been lost and were on strike. So I was

[1] Mencap is a UK charity for people with a learning disability, www.mencap.org.uk

left on my own really! They supported me as friends, they did. They didn't completely leave me in the lurch but they weren't up on stage with me.

I remember that meeting very well. I remember everyone coming to the meeting. There was me, little Richard, on the stage, and the councillor, who was co-chairing the meeting with me, and then one of the top bosses from the council – the man who decided to give the chop to People First. There was another head from social services there. So there was me stuck in a sandwich between the councillors and the heads of social services.

There were some faces that I recognised in the crowd, some friendly faces. There was Louise and our community leader. I was quite pleased to see them there.

It was going to be a very stormy and not very comfortable meeting to chair. I remember the councillor saying to me that it was not going to be easy. She was also new to chairing a meeting, she was. She said, *'This is how we'll do it'*. She said more or less that she would lead the meeting. So the meeting started.

The councillor, who I must say is a nice lady, even though she gave the axe to People First, did quite a lot of the talking in the meeting when people were asking questions and saying some things about what their children were losing. I think the councillors tried to apologise for funding cuts and all that. But in the end I got fed up listening to the councillors witter on a bit. I just knew I had to stand up.

I took the microphone out of the councillor's hand, I did, and stood up. There was a lady sitting next to me; she was one of the heads of Social Services, and another councillor whose job it was to really put the chop in it all. I just had to step out of my role of being co-chair of the Partnership Board, and I said that the council had made a mistake, they had, and not really thought it all through, taking people's services away from them, and I said that, *'I can see more people ending up going to hospital or ending up going into prison 'cos they get stressed and anxious and worried about it all'.*

I had to say what I had to say and stand up for people with learning disabilities. I sort of told the councillors off, I did. I think I also might have told the councillor what I thought of him. I can't remember what I said to him but all I remember was he left the meeting in a huff, he did, because everyone was booing him and cheering me. I think I just said it was wrong what they were doing, cutting People First and cutting the funding from Mencap.

It was quite sad listening to the parents saying how much their child was going to lose with activities being cut. I just came to L'Arche afterwards and people said what a good job I had done at the meeting.

I remember after that meeting I had a very, very bad headache, I did, but I managed to have a glass of wine, a big glass of wine! I needed it after that meeting, just to recover from it all.

CHAPTER 24

A TRUSTEE FOR WALSINGHAM SUPPORT

Me with Heather Benjamin who used to be chair of the committee of Walsingham Support

I am a trustee of Walsingham Support, which is a national charity like L'Arche which supports people with learning disabilities. I'm the representative on their committee, representing people with learning disabilities. I'm the only person on the committee with learning disabilities. I have been doing it now since 2013. I really like being a trustee on their committee because it makes me feel quite important, representing people with learning disabilities. It's important to me that they get their voice heard and it's good that I am on the committee so I can speak up for them and say what I think is right or wrong.

It was Jane, the lady who helps me do the stuff I do for the Lambeth Assembly for People with Learning Disabilities, who knew of this charity. Sadly, Mabel Cooper, the lady with learning disabilities who was on the committee before me, passed away, she did. So Jane thought of me. She used to support Mabel. I never knew Mabel Cooper but I followed in her footsteps and admired her life as she was one of the first campaigners for people with learning disabilities.

Jane just said to me, *'Richard, there's a place come up for someone to be on the committee of Walsingham Support'*. I said, *'Thank you for thinking of me'*. I thought it was a good idea so I said yes straight away, I did.

I went for a meeting up in London to meet Paul Snell, the man in charge of their organisation. I also met the chair of the committee at that time, and the Vice Chair. We met in a very posh place down Pall Mall. We talked about their charity, we did. And we talked a bit about L'Arche and about me. I said I would be interested to be on their committee.

Paul arranged for me to go on two visits to look at their services, he did. So I went with him and we looked at a residential house, we did, and a supported living project. The house was very nice and the flats were very nice. I remember one man very well, I do. He lived in a flat but he didn't have very much sight and couldn't really speak very well. The lady in charge of the project there, and me and Paul went to talk to him. And I said to him, *'Hello, my name's Richard. And I'm going to be on the committee for Walsingham Support'*. He just took me by the arm and started showing me round his flat, he did. I think that they said, *'Oh he likes you, he does'*. So I decided then this is what I needed to do, to be a voice on their committee, to be a voice for people with learning disabilities.

Walsingham Support is like L'Arche because it is a religious charity, it is. It was started up by Paul's father. It was started up to support Paul's brother who has a learning disability. And now they have over 200 people they support over the UK.

My first board meeting was where I sat there just listening. I had to go out the room, I did, for a bit while they approved me to be on the committee. Then I went in, and I'm still there. I will have to do this role now for nine years because that's how long the term is to be on the committee. Every three years you have to be re-elected but after nine years you have to stop.

I do remember at my first meeting, a member of the committee stepped down after doing her term. She got a load of nice leaving presents so I thought to myself, '*Oh, this looks good, it does!*' But seriously I'm honoured to be on their committee, I am.

Now I have some support to help me on the committee for the big meetings. Tim from L'Arche and Jane from Lambeth now take it in turn to support me on the committee, they do. John Sargent, who was then the big boss of L'Arche UK, was pleased that I am on the committee and says that I am doing some good things.

The first board meeting we had, there were a whole lot of new members that meeting and we all had to be approved – about three of us. And we started to talk about finance, money and all that. And I turned round and said, '*Is this when we all start going to prison?*' and they thought that was quite good!

At the first meeting I attended as a full member, they asked me to do the reflection at the start of the meeting and I think I blew them away because I read my Auschwitz paper, I did.[1]

The chair of the committee was a very nice lady, she was. She was a bit like a headmistress, she was. She just liked the meetings to run to time and not to go over. But she always looked out for when I wanted to say something in a meeting and let me speak. She has been involved in lots and lots of companies, she has.

The other trustees are all very nice, they are. Some come from a business background and so know a lot about finances. Some come from the care sector, they do. They all have their own houses, they do, and I live in my own flat with housing benefit, but what I bring to the committee is my knowledge and expertise in learning disabilities, and they all respect me and like me.

Walsingham Support has lots of projects going on. I have to remember to not say things in L'Arche about what Walsingham Support is up to and vice versa. When we go to their meetings we do stop in nice hotels like Laura Ashley Hotel. Let's just put it like this, the places that I have been stopping in with them, no sinks have fallen off the wall![2]

[1] See Chapter 19.
[2] See Chapter 18.

The founder of Walsingham Support went to meet Jean Vanier, the founder of the L'Arche communities, to get some ideas and all that. And I remember at the funeral of Thérèse Vanier,[3] Mark was at the funeral, he was. And he went to say hello to Jean Vanier and said to Jean, as I was there, *'Richard is on our committee, he is'*. And Jean Vanier said, *'You've got a good man on your committee there'*.

Walsingham Support is doing very well and is growing a lot since I've been on the committee. And they respect L'Arche very much, they do.

When I got attacked on the High Street and was feeling quite low about things,[4] I remember that I came back from doing my exercises one evening at Keep Fit with Mencap, and there was a delivery man standing outside the flat, and he said, *'Oh, I've got a box here for Mr Keagan-Bull'*. And I said, *'Oh, that's me, it is'*, but I said, *'I haven't ordered anything'*. So I took the box inside and I opened it up and there was five different boxes of chocolates from Marks and Spencer in there for me from Walsingham Support, just to say they were sorry to hear what happened to me and they hoped I liked the chocolates.

Some years later (in 2017) I went to the requiem mass at Westminster Cathedral for Cardinal Murphy O'Connor and I went with the priest from our community. We represented L'Arche UK. We ended up sitting in the front rows in the VIP area and a man came to sit next to us, and it was Mark from Walsingham Support. So in the end I ended up representing two charities there, I did, and I was just five rows behind Princess Anne. I said, *'We have to get St Paul's Cathedral for my funeral, but not just yet hopefully!'*

[3] Jean Vanier's sister, and the co-founder of L'Arche UK.
[4] See Chapter 34.

CHAPTER 25

HOLIDAYS WITH MENCAP

I remember the local Mencap group in Lambeth. I used to go and do some activities with them sometimes before they closed. I remember their Speaking Up Group. It is a group that met once a month to discuss the activities what were going on in Lambeth and London for people with learning disabilities. I've been on two painting holidays with them, one to the South of France and one to the Caribbean, to Jamaica, yes. They were good holidays, they were, yes. After each holiday we had an exhibition of the work we had done out there, a painting exhibition. People came to have a look at the exhibitions and thought that our work was very nice.

On the holiday in Jamaica, one day we had a look around Bob Marley's tomb and before they let us have a look around it, we had to take our shoes off, we did. But it smelt quite high there with wacky baccy, it did! I think we were all a bit high after looking around there, listening to Bob Marley's music, because in the evening we went down to the beach and we all had cocktails, we did. I had rum in my cocktail, I did, and banana, and now I'm going to say a very rude word I am: the name of my cocktail, it was called a 'Dirty Banana'. The view from the beach where we were sitting, looking across, you could just see in the dark sky in the distance the cruise ships with their lights on. It was beautiful, it was.

When we got back to where we were staying, we all went to bed. I had a very interesting night dream, I did! I think it was to do with the smell of the wacky baccy and the cocktail I had drunk earlier. I dreamt that the Queen had died, she had, and we were all lining the streets watching her funeral and she was in this glass coffin, she was, so people could see her lying there and then the people were throwing flowers at it and all that, and then she stood up, she did, and said, '*I'm alive!*' And then I woke up. I think it was the wacky baccy and the cocktail what did that.

CHAPTER 26

A VOICE FOR PEOPLE WITH LEARNING DISABILITIES

I just want to say, I'm involved in lots of things now, important things like being a trustee on the board of an organisation that supports people with learning disabilities. I want to be a voice for people with learning disabilities, not just a tick in the box to show that they've included someone with a learning disability.

I became an expert by experience of going to visit people with autism in hospitals who end up in a crisis and need some help but ended up in hospital. I was the expert by experience on the CTR reviews for people like that.[1] I did about eight or ten of these, I did. I did a few in a low-grade hospital where we sat down and had the meetings and Jane again supported me to read the files of the person we were talking about. And then the person would sometimes come into the meetings and sometimes not and we would go and see them. 'Cos some of them were in there because they had been sectioned, they had a carer with them. They weren't on their own.

I remember I actually did two without Jane helping me. My mum came with me, she did. Not to be in the meeting but she just came to the hospital where the meeting was taking place. I just remember we were walking down to the hospital and there was a big wall and a big fence. I thought, '*This is like prison, this one is!*' I was a bit scared and thought, '*This is going to be interesting!*'

The ones who were at that hospital were quite high offenders with a learning disability. At the end of the day it was all about working out whether they should be there or in another setting. I remember that the first time I looked at the files without Jane, a commissioner helped me. And I saw where they had come from and it was the first time I had seen the name of a prison. All the other ones just had challenging behaviour and needed some support. All that work, I had to keep it confidential, I did.

[1] Care Treatment Reviews.

The two reviews I did at the high security hospital, even I was escorted to the toilets by one of the guards, I was. I felt very touched and sad about the situations of the people with learning disabilities there and how they had ended up there. But they did nice Danish pastries there!

So after this when I went to the Friendly Group meeting in Lambeth, the lady who was in charge of that meeting said that she had just been given an email because they were looking for some people to be experts by experience on the South East London Transforming Care Partnership. I said, '*Oh, I think I would like to see if I could have a go at doing that*'. So I met some other people, and some family carers who have got loved ones who have been in these situations.

I have met many people now, and seen many things, and been to many countries. I just hope that I am doing some good for people in the things that I do. It's also been good being an advocate because you get to meet people in high places and they get to know you too.

CHAPTER 27

LAMBETH CHAMPION, 2015

I became Chair of the Assembly for People with Learning Disabilities in Lambeth. It used to be the Partnership Board. Because of funding cuts it stopped, and then the Assembly was born.

And a few years later I was nominated for an award in Lambeth, I was.

I just had my birthday party what my mum very kindly organised for me at home. It was the day afterwards – I was just looking at my emails on my iPad, there was an email from the Mayor of Lambeth's office. It said, *'We would like to invite you to the Community Awards Ceremony at the Royal Festival Hall. But not only would we like to invite you but you have been nominated for an award and shortlisted. You might want to get a speech prepared. You can invite one guest and the person who nominated you is Jane Abraham'.* So I just rushed up to show my mum the email. My mum saw the email and said, *'That's good!'* And I think I showed the email to my dad. And I had to respond to the email to say that I would be coming. And then I phoned Jane. She said, *'Wow! Oh good!'* She was pleased that I found out. Then she told me of all the other people who had nominated me, people from L'Arche, from Lambeth Mencap, and the head of Social Services for people with learning disabilities.

That evening after I spoke with Jane, I was talking to my mum and she said, *'You being nominated has put the icing on the cake for this weekend. It was just a shame we heard about it the day after the birthday because it would have been nice to tell people'.*

Two days before the award ceremony I got another email from the Mayor of Lambeth and this time it said, *'Dear Friend, if you would like, you could invite someone else to come for the award ceremony, you can'.* So I phoned home and spoke to my mum and said, *'Would dad like to come to the award ceremony now?'* She asked him and he said yes, he would.

Two friends helped me to look the part, they did. I was all dressed up smart, I was. I went to the Royal Festival Hall with Jane and met my mum and dad.

As we went to sit down, the person from Lambeth Council hosting the event asked us if we wanted a glass of wine to drink. I stood and looked out the window of the fifth floor holding my glass of wine looking out across the Thames. You could see the Houses of Parliament and I remembered being there for a talk by the founder of L'Arche to the members of the Lords a few weeks before and I felt very proud.

We went back to the table with the posh tablecloth on it and the ceremony was just about to start. There was a councillor sitting at our table, and they said, '*Would you all please stand with a glass in your hand to toast the Mayor of Lambeth as he comes in?*' So the Mayor of Lambeth walks in in his robes with his white gloves on and his chain of office. The mace was in front of him. So it was all very posh, it was. We all sat down at our tables and the Mayor said, '*Everyone who has been nominated has done well to be nominated*'.

My award was about the fifth or sixth. They had different people giving awards to people. They had the borough commander of Lambeth; he gave an award to somebody. I had two ladies from the Terence Higgins Trust to give me my award. When it came to my award they read out all the names of the nominees who were shortlisted. I did know one of the ladies in my category, which was a bit difficult. My heart was going boom tiddi boom tiddi boom tiddi **boom**! And I held my mum's hand. And they got the gold envelope out, they did, the two ladies, and they said:

The winner is...

Richard Keagan-Bull...

for keeping Lambeth healthy.

I was speechless and broke down in tears. Me mum looked at Jane and they both had tears in their eyes and couldn't believe what had just happened. So I had to walk onto the stage, I did. I made my speech what came out of my head.

Don't put us away!

I said that I was very proud to receive this award. I can't remember it quote for quote but I said, '*It is very difficult in the world to have a*

learning disability. I just want to say thank you to those who started up L'Arche so people can live like I do independently in their own flats'. And I said, 'There's two people sitting over there' – meaning my mum and dad – 'who were told when I was born – and my brother, not to worry about us, just to put us to one side, like'. I think I said thank you to them. I hope I did. Then I said, 'I just want to do something now', I did. I said, 'I can't do it in front of you, Mr Mayor', I said, 'Sorry'. And the borough commander was sitting in front of me and I said, 'I can't do it in front of you', I said – he was all dressed up in his uniform. So we were on the fifth floor of the Royal Festival Hall so I went to the window, and I stuck two fingers up out the window and I said, 'That's to the professionals who told my mum and dad they could just put us away and forget about us!' I don't mince my words, I don't. I just say it as it is. By that time I think everyone was crying and laughing at the same time at my speech.

But I could not get off the stage because my legs had gone to jelly, they had. So one of the Lambeth councillors and me and my mum went out the room a bit so I could just pull myself together again. And the man who was in charge of hanging up the coats, he said, 'Well done! Well deserved!' he said. He gave me a glass of water to drink, he did.

And afterwards we went back in to listen to the other people who were getting awards. And then after that it was just like being at the Oscars, it was! I had to get my picture done professionally for Lambeth, I did, with all the other winners. There were seven winners, I think. And we all stood there having our picture taken. And then I had my picture taken with the Mayor on my own. I also met the Borough Commander, who said, 'I want to meet your mum and dad'. So my mum and dad and me had our picture taken with the Borough Commander.

I phoned Hazel but she was busy having a Skype call with America – she spoke to me anyway and the people on the other end of her call all heard that I had won an award and how excited Hazel was for me. Then I said I had to go as there were so many people wanting to congratulate me!

So at the end of the evening I came back to West Norwood with my certificate and my trophy in my bag and my badge saying Lambeth Champion. My mum and dad went home with a big bunch of flowers, which they gave them. I had a text from my dad when they were on the train to say that my mum's phone had died with all the texting and messaging she'd done telling people that I had won the award! I feel happy when my mum is proud of the things I do. And my dad.

I've now got the certificate on my wall and my award on a shelf in my room so people can see it when they come into my flat. I feel quite honoured, I do. I feel like I have made my name in Lambeth, I have.

PART IV

BELONGING

CHAPTER 28

40TH BIRTHDAY PARTY

Me and Hazel were just sitting down to write about my 40th birthday party.

Writing my life story with Hazel

This is when I should explain how I wrote this book. It started off when Hazel and I were talking and she said, *'Why don't you write down your memories, so you have something to remember your life story?'*. So then Hazel and I arranged some sessions where I would tell her my thoughts and memories and she would write them down for me. We worked on it on and off for a number of years. It got bigger and bigger. We thought it would be a nice thing to make into a book for my mum.

We enjoyed it, we did. It was entertaining, it was, us working together. I would tease her and make fun of all her funny teas and recipes that she used to have, like nettles and seaweed and all that.

So for the story of my 40th birthday party, I'm just sitting here waiting for a Skype call because Hazel's having a bit of a funny day today because she can't remember what she's doing and while I'm just sitting here Hazel's eating some peculiar porridge with some funny things in it. I like my porridge with just milk and brown sugar. I don't think I could cope with the soya milk. Plain and simple. And I don't want to ask what's in that funny-looking water she's going to drink now! With some cider vinegar and honey in it! I'm just wondering where her broomstick is! I don't really want to ask what's in it and it's chucking it down with rain outside, it is. I even had to make my own cup of tea this morning and there was no milk for it. So that's that.

My 40th birthday party

My 40th! For some reason I decided that I wanted to celebrate my 40th birthday party and go big. I started to have some planning meetings to plan it with my support team at the time. I remember they had some team meetings to talk about it. My support manager was getting a bit worried and nervous that it was going to be quite big.

How I wanted my 40th birthday party, the things what I wanted, what was special to me: of course I wanted people from L'Arche to be there, but I also wanted some friends who had been good to my mum and dad when me and my brother were growing up, who'd been very supportive to us, to the whole family.

I remember some particular people we sent invitations to, who very kindly came to my party. Sue and Peter: Sue is a very close school friend of my mother; they've known each other for a very long time. Philip and I are the same age as their two sons, well near enough. They came all the way from the Channel Islands to help me celebrate my 40th birthday party. And we made it quite special as my mum and dad, and Philip and Sue and Peter stayed on the South Bank for a couple of nights in a university accommodation which my mum found.

I was also very touched by somebody else who came to my 40th birthday party. Alex his name is. And his wife came. When I was a young boy, a little boy, Alex and I were neighbours; our back fences backed onto each other. I think I really got to know Alex because we went to Cubs together, we did. We started to get to know each other a bit. What my mum tells me about it is, how we got to know each other quite well, is that his mum came to my house once and asked her, *'Would you like some apples or something?'* As my mum explained to her, we grew apples and pears so we got apples quite regularly. I think it turned out that they wanted to invite me to go round to Alex's house for tea. They wanted to help me read and write, they did. All I can really remember about going to Alex's house now is that we used to dress up and put shows on for his mum and dad.

Alex and I lost contact when I went to boarding school. For quite a few years when I used to come home to my mum and dad to see them, we used to drive past the house where Alex used to live with his mum and dad. And I used to say, *'I wonder what happened to Alex and where he is now'*. Like my mum is, she started to do a bit of investigation, she did. And she got in touch with someone who used to live by him and she got his telephone number, I think. I think I hadn't seen him for about 30 years, or for a very long time, and my mum phoned him and he said, *'Of course I'd like to see Richard!'* So the first time I went to see him, my mum came with me, she did. He opened the door, he did, and my mum said, '*He hasn't changed one bit, he hasn't, just a bit older!*' So we had a good catch up, we did, about where our lives had gone and all that. So I was very touched when he came all the way from Essex to my 40th birthday party. I remember what Alex and his wife bought me: they bought me a wallet, they did.

And now I have to tell you about another lady who came to my birthday party. Beth, her name is. Beth is a lady who used to go to my college, the Derwen. Her disability is Down's Syndrome. We both had little flats at the college, we did. We used to work with each other in the coffee shop. I used to go and call her to come to work on my way to the coffee shop, which could be quite a long process, 'cos if we were late getting to the coffee shop they used to take time off our coffee break – that's how strict they were at the Derwen. In the end I used to say to Beth, '*I've got to go now Beth as I don't want to lose time off my coffee break*'. Sometimes we used to turn up together and most of the time she used to turn up an hour later, she did. Sometimes poor Beth used to lose all her break time, she did. But I think her mum and dad were very pleased that I took the time just to make sure she was okay. So I was really quite touched that they came all the way from Birmingham to my birthday party, Beth and her parents. Beth would not be able to travel independently like me on her own, she would need some support, and nor could she live on her own like I have my own flat. Now and again to this day Beth and I keep in touch, usually via her dad.

My good friend, Carmel, from L'Arche also came to my party. She bought me some nice ties for my shirts. I became friends with Carmel when I first came to the community, because we were in the same holiday group. She really wanted to do what I was doing, living independently in my own flat on my own. And now she is! She trusts me. Sometimes she is in a good mood, and sometimes she is just happy to talk to me but no one else.

Hazel, in a speech, she read out the piece what I wrote about Auschwitz, she did. A special friend of mine back in Essex who makes cakes, I wanted her to make my cake, I did. It came by special delivery by two good friends of my mum who brought it by car to the party.

I just have to say that the team from L'Arche made the church hall look very beautiful, they did, just how I wanted it. We bought some nice cloths to make into tablecloths, we did. They were white, they were. I've still got them to this day, I have. We had gold and blue balloons on each table, we did, because blue is my favourite colour.

They arranged that Philip, my brother, would bring in my birthday cake and everybody sang '*Happy Birthday*' to me. It was a good time had by all, I think. We had some music in the background, we did.

At the end of the party I felt quite happy – I guess I thought, '*That's the 30s gone, now the 40s are here!*' I felt quite happy. I'd made a big step in my life from moving from the college to living in my own flat. I felt quite good really. I felt quite honoured and proud that so many people had come to my party, to my quite special day. It's good to look back at all the nice birthday cards I got.

CHAPTER 29

MEMORIES OF A ROYALIST

Charles and Diana's wedding

My first memory of anything to do with the royal family was on the eve of the royal wedding of Prince Charles and Lady Diana Spencer in 1981 when I was ten. We went to watch the royal fireworks display in London. There was me, my mum and my brother and a couple of friends of ours and a couple more children. We all went up as a group. It was so busy in London. People were just sitting in the streets and parks, waving flags, all camping out for the wedding the next day. I don't remember too much about the actual fireworks but it was quite late when we came home. It was so crowded, flags flying – it was a real party atmosphere, it was.

I think we just got to the train station to go home, just as the last train was leaving. Auntie Brenda said to me, '*If we miss the train, we'll have to stay up in London*'.

The next day, on the actual wedding, Auntie Brenda and her son and some other people all came to our bungalow and we all watched the royal wedding together. That's my memory of that wedding.

Birth of Prince William

My next memory is being at school, Trueloves, my boarding school, and Matron told us that Prince William had been born, or rather that a boy had been born. We all had a glass of Coca-Cola and biscuits to celebrate the birth of the future king. We had a bit of a party.

I went up to London with my mum and my brother Philip, and my granny might have been with us. She normally tagged along with us when we went out. We went to see the gifts, the presents what people had sent Prince Charles and Lady Diana for their baby William, at Kensington Palace, the toys and everything.

Royal funerals

My first big memory was the funeral of Lord Mountbatten, which was on my birthday I think. He was Prince Charles' great uncle, I think. We'll have to check that one or I might end up in the Tower and have my head chopped off!

I remember going up to London after the Queen Mother died and queuing to see her lying in state. I remember there were crowds upon crowds of people. The prime minister of the time didn't think anyone would turn out but how wrong did he get that?! That was Tony Blair. I'd better not get too political had I?! I do think that if you go and vote you can have a say in things, but if you don't vote, you can't say you've had your say. It's your way of saying what you want for the country and how you want to see the country run. I definitely vote each time. I use my right to vote.

We queued for four hours just to walk around her coffin. There were some quite elderly people who were queuing and everyone was just talking about the royal family and about the Queen Mother. They remembered how she stayed in London in the war and didn't leave. She was a real hero to them in the war.

I remember another memory about the Queen Mother. One year my mum and I came up to Clarence House, the Queen Mother's house, because it was her birthday. There were crowds of people standing outside and I think that we got to see her – just her hat. I think she was sitting on a golf buggy – and there was a balloon on the buggy. One of the police officers said to us, *'When she used to go on holiday to Scotland, she used to send the police a card to say thank you for looking after her'.*

William and Kate's wedding

I guess my recent memory is driving up to London the eve of the wedding of William and Kate in April 2011, with Hazel and some others. We drove up the Mall and people were camping on the streets. They were all happy. People were pressing their hooters. We were shouting out the car saying hello to people. We drove up to Buckingham Palace and there was all hooters going off up there, there was.

We stopped at a pub nearby where the drinks were quite expensive. We found out that the hotel where Kate Middleton was stopping the night before her wedding was quite close. We walked to the hotel. It was such a party atmosphere, it was! There was this really camp TV reporter from one of the American networks and it was just funny watching him reporting on what Kate's hair would look like and what she would be wearing, and what Prince William would be wearing. Everyone, including the police standing there, were in fits of giggles listening to him. That made our evening, it did.

Procession of the Order of the Royal Garter

Hazel and I were lucky to get two tickets from a neighbour of Hazel's to go to the procession of the Order of the Royal Garter. We took a train to Windsor Castle. It was a really hot day. There was big queues of people waiting to get into the castle to watch the procession. We were standing there for a long time waiting to get in. I had my chair with me to sit down, I did. After our long queue we got in there, we did, and we were told where we could go and sit. We just sat and stood for hours waiting for something to happen. We saw soldiers starting to march up and down the road taking their places for the parade. Then the band started to play some music. Then we started to see people walking into the chapel. We were looking to see who we could recognise.

Then some big cars came along with Camilla Parker Bowles in, and Sophie Wessex, Prince Edward's wife. There were some other members of the royal family in cars, with their big hats on. But we knew when it was a member of the royal family as the soldiers kept shouting, '*Salute!*'

Then we saw the procession of the members of the Order of the Royal Garter, the knights and ladies, walking up in their fine outfits. Behind them we saw the Queen in the middle, Prince Charles and Prince William. Prince William was holding her hand. The Duke of Edinburgh was poorly in hospital so he couldn't be there. Then they all went into the chapel.

There were beefeaters in their uniforms, soldiers in their smart uniforms, there were military bands, horses and carriages, all the lords and ladies in their velvet outfits – and I turned to Hazel and

Me watching the Procession of the Order of the Royal Garter at Windsor Castle

said, '*They could do with you throwing a few of your cloths around!*' She laughed. Hazel uses a lot of coloured cloths when we do liturgies and workshops. I have told her that when she dies, we will cover her coffin in rainbow cloths!

They went into the chapel and we could hear the music being played. We had the service in booklets so we could follow it if we wanted to. I think they were in there for about an hour. We could hear them playing the National Anthem. We could hear the airplanes flying to Heathrow Airport because it was quite close. I hope the Queen has double-glazing or she'll never get a good night's sleep!

So we saw them come out the chapel; this time they were in state coaches, they were, with the horsemen all looking posh and the Queen sitting in the back of the carriage. And they came past us in their carriages. But it was a case of, if you blinked, you missed them.

We saw John Major, Princess Anne, Princess Alexandra, the Duke of Kent, the Duke of Gloucester, Prince Andrew and Prince Edward. We saw them all go back and then we walked out the castle gates, we did.

I was quite thirsty but we were in a bit of a time rush as I had to get to London Euston as I was going to Manchester Piccadilly to go to a meeting for L'Arche, I was. I think that Hazel was just wanting to get a cup of tea in a cheap and cheerful café but I must admit I think I saw the most expensive tea room with table cloths on the tables and china tea cups. I said, *'That's where I want to go for a cup of tea'*. Once we were there we ordered a full cream tea. Poor Hazel must have thought, *'Oh deary me!'* But it was very good and really needed! Lots of rich-looking people kept coming in and there was us poor people sitting there enjoying it all! And we had a very nice day.

CHAPTER 30

GREENBELT FESTIVAL

Me at Greenbelt with David Stephenson and Hazel Bradley

The first year I went to Greenbelt,[1] I didn't really know what to expect. But I was pleased that I was staying in a nice hotel type of thing and not in a tent! I remember we arrived there, we did, and we all met with the other L'Arche groups in the rest room for people with disabilities that L'Arche started and ran at Greenbelt. Hazel met us there. We all said hello to everybody and there was a nice couple there who made sandwiches and rolls for us to eat.

The next day we all met and Hazel stood up in the middle, she did, and said, *'We need to get ourselves organised to do a mime'*. Then all these cloths came out and bowls and jugs and sticks, and all sorts of things. We rehearsed the mime which we were going to do. In the afternoon we did the mime for about 150 people, and ended it with

[1] A UK arts, faith and justice Christian festival.

Me in a mime of the Raising of Lazarus at Greenbelt with Terri Clements, L'Arche Kent and Kathy Kramers, L'Arche Bognor – 2008

the Washing of the Feet. It was fun to take part in it. I remember that the people who came were very moved when we did the Washing of the Feet in our little groups. Someone was in a wheelchair and got out of it to wash someone's feet in his group with the help of his support worker. The lady who had her feet washed by someone in a wheelchair was moved to tears.

Afterwards we had lunch together sitting together in a room looking out over Cheltenham Racecourse. Some of us had sandwiches and some of us had weird-looking food to eat. I said, 'What's that you're eating Hazel?' and she said, 'They're mung bean sprouts'. They looked like if you put water on them you could grow them! She does eat some peculiar stuff, really funny things. But I'm sure they're doing her some good!

When we go to Greenbelt we give so much in our liturgies and people really appreciate them and sometimes come away with tears in their eyes and want to know more about L'Arche. Some have even come back as assistants. I like being in front of the house, acting and speaking and performing.

What's good about going to Greenbelt is that you get to listen to quite a lot of speakers, but what's hard is there is quite a lot of walking and you have to take your own seat to sit on. After the first year I got my own seat to sit down on! You couldn't miss anyone from L'Arche as we had our bright orange T-shirts on.

In 2013, I got asked to come to Greenbelt to help to give a talk about how people with learning disabilities can be welcomed in churches. Before we went to Greenbelt we went to visit Lucy Winkett, the lady vicar who was going to chair our panel. She does 'Thought for the Day' sometimes on Radio 4. There was myself, Hazel, David the vicar from my church and Lucy from St James Church, Piccadilly. We met her in her office. We talked about what we were going to talk about on the stage at Greenbelt. I think that me and Lucy hit it off, we did!

The next day we arrived in the tent 'The Sitting Room' where we were going to do the talk. It was all set up like a sitting room. We sat on a sofa and they had these pretend tea cups and saucers but they were glued together so you couldn't use them.

Then we talked about our experiences, how we find church.
I remember saying how I went to church and it was the final of the Australian Open and Andy Murray was playing. I was telling people that I was more interested in listening to the results on my mobile than listening to the sermon! I didn't know that Gill, the curate from our church, was in the tent listening to our talk. She was with her husband George, who later became our community leader. So hopefully our talk encouraged him to become our community leader.

I remember saying in the talk everybody has the right, and everybody should be able to go to church, whether they are quiet or not, to be able to take part in the service and to be seen by people and to be part of the community of the church. When the vicar tries to include people with disabilities in the church service it is good. David (our vicar) used to say to Maggie if she spoke out loud, he would say, *'That's right, Maggie'.* He would include people and not leave them at the back. He did go to people's level when he gave communion. He used to give people hugs, he did. I was a server in the church and David used to – whenever I wanted to read out the notices at the end of the Sunday service, he was quite happy for me to do it. He was very keen on getting me involved in the PCC.[2] I became a member.

---

[2] Parochial Church Council.

I've seen sometimes in other churches when people have been left at the back and not always included. I think people should be included.

I think the talk went down very well. People were very interested and did have some questions. I just hope that from the talk we were giving it gave people and vicars a better understanding of people with learning disabilities and letting them be part of the service and not making them sit in a room on their own.

Afterwards one day when I was at home with my mum and dad, Lucy Winkett was doing 'Thought for the Day' on Radio 4 and mum shouted, *'Oh, one of your friends is on the radio now, she is!'*

CHAPTER 31

ADVENTURES IN GHANA AND COLOMBIA

Ghana, 2016

Jane, who helps me to do the work I do here in Lambeth, also spends part of her time in Ghana because her husband is Ghanaian and they do some business out there. She invited me to go and spend some time with her and her husband in Ghana. And to do some work out there and to meet people with learning disabilities whose lives are different from what we live here in England.

It has to be said that in Africa that if you have a learning disability it's seen as a curse on your family. So sadly there are lots of people with disabilities living on the streets. I saw this both in Ghana and Colombia, I did, and in India. That made me feel quite sad and upset and made me feel how lucky we are here in England.

There are also many good projects in Ghana which Jane took me to see what good things they are doing for people. There were some schools for people with special needs. I talked to people about life here in England for people with disabilities. I met some nice people.

The food was interesting, it was; some nice and some not so nice. It was different to England. We had air conditioning on in the house. There were power cuts. They had monsoons so when it rained it just came down really heavy. It was just a completely different way of life to how I live here in England.

It was very nice of Jane to invite me to go to Ghana and to get to see life there and how things are different. I got to know Jane through my work in Lambeth and how she supports me through her paid work but she has become a good friend and is always on the lookout for jobs for me to do.

Colombia, 2019

A man called Alonso who used to work in my community who is from Colombia was busy setting up a project in Colombia a bit like L'Arche. He came back to London and visited our community and he invited me to go to Colombia to see what he was setting up because he thought it would be interesting for me to see what he was doing there. So we arranged the trip, we did. And he thought it would be a good idea to go while there was a lady from L'Arche Kent also going to be out there at the same time. It would be better for me so we could do things together and just have a bit of company for when Alonso was working.

I flew to Colombia single-handedly on my own, with a bit of assistance from the airport; I was put in a wheelchair, whisked through the airport and then about 12 hours later arrived in Bogota in Colombia. The flight itself was the first time I had been on a long long flight on my own. I have been on long flights with my family but this was the first time I had been on my own.

Me arriving after my long flight to Colombia

I got put in a wheelchair again at Colombia and whisked through the airport. I met Alonso, who had a long conversation in Spanish saying, 'Richard can walk, he can. He doesn't need a wheelchair'. The first thing Alonso and I did was to send a picture to my mum and to various people just to say I had arrived. And we had to walk to get another plane, we did, to where we were going to stay. I went to see the work what Alonso is doing in Colombia. I stayed with his family, I did.

The days I wasn't working with Alonso, I spent some time looking around but the work that Alonso was doing was very interesting. He arranged for us to have three days, just him and me in the jungle. So we spent three days in the jungle and swimming in the Atlantic in a nice retreat place. I think it was three hours away from Panama. My room where I was living was very close to a pond where there were two crocodiles. It was quite eerie. I didn't see them but knew they were there.

Colombia was a big adventure and I enjoyed it. It was good to get to know the lady from L'Arche Kent. Sometimes things got a little stressful and she helped me to just calm down a bit.

Missing my friends' funerals

Before I went to Columbia I knew that two of my friends in the community, Carol and Michelle, had died, and I was going to be away for their funerals. We had already booked my travel and couldn't change it. I kept my watch on English time so when I landed in Columbia I knew it was time for Carol's funeral in England. I knew everyone would be going to the church and my mum would be arriving there. She wore a hat, she did, because Carol liked hats and everyone was asked to wear one.

Alonso's nephew, he looked after me the first evening. We went to the church and I lit a candle for Carol, I did. Then we went back to their flat and I slept and slept and slept. I was in Colombia for Michelle's funeral too. Some of the funeral was filmed and put on YouTube. Alonso and I watched it on YouTube so we saw what was going on, we did.

It was quite sad to miss the funeral. It was weird and quite moving and touching to see what we saw on YouTube, all my friends in the community. We normally all get together for funerals in the community. We all become one big community, we do. I think that's very nice how we do funerals in L'Arche, celebrating people's lives. People who may not have had a good life before L'Arche but in L'Arche, when they die we celebrate them we do. And we have nice cake too!

CHAPTER 32

BELONGING

I like being supported by L'Arche. You become part of an international community. When the sun's setting on our communities in Europe, it's rising on the communities in Australia and New Zealand.

Everybody deserves to be loved. Everybody has a gift. My gift is that I'm quite good at standing on a stage and making speeches. I can tell the story of L'Arche and spread the word about it. Being an ambassador for L'Arche has taken me to Kolkata, Canada, Italy and Belgium. Others might not be able to talk like me, but perhaps they're good at dancing, singing, painting. The beauty of the founder Jean Vanier was that he saw that everybody has a gift, and everybody should be able to shine their light.

In 2017 it was a very big day for us in L'Arche London, opening our refurbished new office and workshop building. It's taken quite a while to get to where we are now. I made a speech, I did. They put my speech on Facebook.[1]

I said how Thérèse Vanier founded L'Arche in the UK and Jean Vanier founded L'Arche worldwide. It's thanks to them for opening the doors for many people with learning disabilities across the world who have the right to be seen and to be heard, not to be stuck in a corner, you know, patted on the head, that type of thing, which did happen to us at my old college once it did, yes.

L'Arche is also about friendships and belonging. At the end of the day that is quite important. At the end of the day you don't want just to get support to make sure you're not dead, that you haven't fallen off your perch. What's important is being part of a nice community, where you get people around you who care about you, not just when they're being paid for it; they care about who you are all the time.

So, you know, L'Arche may not be very big. But what is nice about being part of L'Arche is that we all get together for birthday parties and celebrations, any excuse for a party really. And you are allowed to have people's telephone numbers and all that.

[1] www.facebook.com/watch/?extid=SEO----&v=919515471506791

PART V

MY NAME ON THE DOOR

CHAPTER 33

FINDING A PROPER JOB

Some years ago now, I decided I didn't want to keep going to college. I decided that I had enough of going to college. Because I moved away from living at a college, I did, to get away from all that a bit. So I decided I wanted to get some paid work if I could. So Louise and me got in touch with Mencap Pathways and we went to have a meeting with them. We had a meeting with the manager. I said that I wanted to see if I could get a part-time job. And so he took down all my details, and Louise said I was good at cooking and could make cakes and all that. We explained to him about the college I used to go to, the Derwen. He found a job for me to do. But I think, if I remember rightly, it was going to be full time, every day of the week, to work in a school's kitchen.

I went there with the Mencap manager to try it out, working in the kitchen. The first day wasn't too bad. It was a job to be a porter in the kitchen. I think the children were about four or five. I think they were infants, young children, they were. The second day I wasn't really sure if I would like working there because the people I worked with weren't quite friendly really.

I think the third day I made my decision, or maybe the fourth day I made my decision. And I met the manager in the usual place in Tulse Hill where we took the bus to go to do my work. And I just said to him it wasn't really the job I wanted to do. I don't think I went to the job that day. He did say to me it was fine, even though he could have put a tick in his box that he had got me a job, which is what he wanted.

Cleaning job at Plough Studios

I don't think I heard from him for a couple of months. And then he phoned me up at my flat, he did. And he said, 'Richard, I think I've found for you the perfect job. There's a film studio, a photo studio where they do some filming and they would really like to have a cleaner come up for just a couple of hours a week'. And he said, 'It might be just what you are looking for as it is part time and not full time', he said.

We went to visit Plough Studios and we met the person in charge of the studios, Tim. For the first few weeks a man from Mencap called James was going to come with me just for the first six weeks just to help me do the work so I could get into it – like a work buddy.

So then I went to do my cleaning job once a fortnight on a Tuesday. In the beginning James would meet me there. It was also a job share. Another man with learning disabilities went one week and I went the next week. After about six weeks James didn't come every time with me, he didn't. And then they just left me on my own to do the cleaning job.

It used to be that I would get there, Tim would show me where to clean and he would say to me, *'Oh if you want to have a cup of tea you can, and you can make it while you are working'*. I would do my cleaning job for two hours and then Tim made me a cup of tea and we would sit down and have a bit of a chat. And the best thing was that on the pay slip I should be paid £15 for two hours but I sometimes got £20, I did.

I really enjoyed going to work at the studio and cleaning. It was nice to get out and about and see what was going on in the studios. Sometimes they had fashion shoots in the studios going on there. And they had shops like Marks and Spencer take photos of things what they were selling. And sometimes they had some celebrities go there and I ended up cleaning the toilet where certain celebrities have sat, like Ant and Dec and Holly Willoughby.

We kept having a joke when I went to the studios because they knew how much I liked Susan Boyle and I kept asking, *'Has Susan Boyle been brought in yet?'*

And Tim from Plough Studios, he just one day said to me, *'Oh Richard, I was talking to my mum who goes to church'*, and he was saying that *'I have this man who comes to work at Plough Studios who gets support from L'Arche'*, and he said that *'Next time she was stopping in London with him she would like to have a look around L'Arche because she had heard about it'*. So they did. They came and had a cup of tea with us.

And also Tim was very impressed with all the things what I did, like going to India and Atlanta. And I said to him, *'Maybe it would be me coming to the studios one day to have a photo shoot of me!'*

I should also say that when I went to France with Lambeth Mencap to do a painting holiday out there, that the art teacher for Lambeth

Mencap was just telling me about the exhibition she was planning to do for the French trip and she was hoping to make some of the pictures look a bit more professional and nice, so I said to her that I could ask where I do my cleaning job if Mencap could use the studios. So I asked Tim at Plough Studios, I did. I explained to him about our holidays and what we did out there. He said to me, *'Richard, get them to give me a call and I will see what I can do'*. And he very kindly let Lambeth Mencap use one of the studios on a Saturday when he wasn't very busy, free of charge. It had to be when he didn't have paying clients paying lots of money. I feel I just want to say, *'It's nice to get on a bus on a Tuesday and go to do a job where you are appreciated'*.

Tim took a lot of pictures of tennis players and he let me have one of his tennis books for my dad's 80th birthday. My dad's a real tennis fan. I held a cheese and wine party for Walsingham Support, I did, and we had a raffle, and Tim gave me a big signed poster of Andy Murray, he did.

So that's my cleaning job then.

CHAPTER 34

GETTING PUNCHED

I was just on my way to go and do my one day of work a week at Plough Studios, doing my cleaning job. I was just walking to the bus stop, which is at the bottom of my road. And I was just standing there and there was a man just walking up and down the street. And just out of nowhere, he came up to me and punched me, he did. It was a hard punch. It wasn't soft. I could really feel it. And naturally I was a bit shocked and a bit upset. I was very shocked and very upset! I went to the L'Arche office because I knew it was a safe place to go to. And I just walked into the community – I think I looked a bit stressed and they saw me and I told them what happened and I burst into tears. So they said, '*Sit there Richard*'. And they said, '*We need to call the police*'. So they did. And then they made me a cup of tea, they did.

The police came to the community and I think before even they took the statement they said they had picked someone up, they had. 'Cos it turned out it wasn't just me who got punched. Someone else got injured. The policewoman, one of these special constables, she gave me a cuddle, she did. I remember I took a picture of the man I did, with my phone. The policeman said, '*That's very good Richard, but it could have been a bit dangerous if he had seen you take the picture*'.

First of all, the man appeared in court and denied it, he did. The police phoned me up and told me. I was in L'Arche Manchester on a visit, I was, doing some work for L'Arche UK. I got the phone call and I just burst into tears when the police told me on the phone. Then the person from L'Arche Manchester that I was with, she talked to them, she did, because I just couldn't cope with it. I don't think they really understood that I have a learning disability.

Back in London me and my key worker at the time had to go to Croydon. We went on a tour around the courts so I could just get a look at what it would look like when I went to give my evidence in court. My key worker pointed out to the lady in court that it would be better for me to give it by video link, which had already been planned. And then she started asking me some questions. And I couldn't answer the questions very well what she was asking me. And my key worker said to me afterwards, '*They were testing you to see how good you would be giving evidence in court*'. And he said, '*I don't think it's going to happen, I don't*'.

So a few weeks later, the police dropped the case because they didn't think I would be a good witness. I think that was what it was. And I think they made some mistakes in the evidence. So the man got off, he did. I was very cross and upset that the man got off. I told everyone about it. I didn't keep it quiet.

And life goes on. I was a bit nervous about living in my flat, and living independently. It did shake me up. But as they say, I'm still here to tell the tale.

CHAPTER 35

THE MAN WHO FOUNDED L'ARCHE

I thought I had finished the book but now I want to add some thoughts about the man who founded L'Arche.

My memories of Jean Vanier when he was alive

I didn't know who Jean Vanier was until I really became part of the L'Arche community in London. People in the community told me who he was and how he had started L'Arche. I thought, '*He sounds an interesting guy*'. I first met him in Durham at a L'Arche regional gathering in the UK not so long after I came to the community. I thought what he had done setting up all these communities around the world was a wonderful thing and that he was a man who was very much loved and respected.

The next time I met him was in Kolkata, India. I had dinner with him there. I was honoured, I was. Not everyone in L'Arche was invited to dinner with Jean Vanier!

Another time I went to Trosly, the first L'Arche community in France, with Heather, who was responsible for communications in L'Arche UK. The trip was a thank you present from L'Arche UK for all the work I had done setting up the National Speaking Group. We all had our picture taken with Jean Vanier, we did. It was like queuing up at Selfridges to have your photo taken with Father Christmas! We just sat there for five minutes, and when the picture was taken you had to get up and go back to our seats. This was how important Jean Vanier was. People from other countries were in tears, those who hadn't seen him before. They were so pleased to be in his presence.

Then me and my mum were invited to go on a silent retreat in Trosly. Jean Vanier was the speaker. It was quite emotional and powerful listening to him speak. But I have to say, it was a silent retreat, but me and my mum and some assistants from other communities did find some places to speak!

When I got my award in Lambeth, Jean sent me a message saying, *'Congratulations!'* I thought it was a real honour that he did that. It's nice that he remembered who I was, especially as there are so many people around the world who get support from L'Arche.

Then in 2014, Thérèse Vanier, his sister, died. I saw Jean at the funeral in Canterbury Cathedral. I carried the cross into the cathedral and led the procession. I can see my mum sitting there now with tears in her eyes, thinking, *'I'm proud of you'*. I felt it was a big honour to carry the cross in the cathedral and to hear the organ. It was quite something. Jean gave me a hug and said, *'Thank you for doing that, for carrying the cross'*. I think he was quite emotional because it was his big sister's funeral.

In 2015, Jean Vanier was honoured with a big award, the Templeton Prize.[1] The night before he got it, I went to a real posh meal with some other people from our community and there were people from other communities around the world. Some important people who had already received this award were at the meal as well. I was sitting next to someone who had an airport named after him. That was how important this meal was. We were eating real fancy food. It was all lah-di-dah and weird. Not what I am used to! I'm used to food like steak and chips or fish and chips! The waiters all put the food down at the same time. One nodded and then they all put the food down and we all had our own waiter. It was all posh and not cor blimey like I'm used to!

The next day it was an early start as we had to go to a secret location. A taxi came to pick me up from my flat and we drove into London. There were lots of TV cameras there. It was for the press announcement about the award. It was all top secret. I wasn't allowed to tell anyone where I was going or what I was doing. There was a man from the BBC there, Edward Stourton, he was. They made the

---

[1] The **Templeton Prize** is an annual award granted to a living person *'whose exemplary achievements advance philanthropic vision: harnessing the power of the sciences to explore the deepest questions of the universe and humankind's place and purpose within it'* (www.templetonprize.org/templeton-prize-history).

announcement that Jean Vanier had won the Templeton Prize. The announcement was being filmed live across the world. Then there was a question-and-answer session. I asked a question: *'What's the future for L'Arche?'* Jean Vanier smiled and pointed at me. He said, *'You're the future of L'Arche!'* I thought, *'Thank you! That's a great big thing to say to me!'* But what he actually meant was that he was passing on the baton to us and it's up to us to see L'Arche grow in the future.

In 2017, I went to the film premiere of *Summer in the Forest*, a film about Jean Vanier and L'Arche. Jean Vanier was there. The Queen saw the film, and she asked whether she could meet Jean Vanier to talk to him. She had known him 70 years ago when he was in the Navy and he had looked after her and Princess Margaret on a trip to South Africa. So Jean came over to Buckingham Palace, dressed in the blue coat he always wore, and when the Queen saw him she had tears in her eyes. Jean said he could see something really special in the Queen. I bet she saw something special in him too.

Afterwards he came to visit us in L'Arche London. It was all last minute because we weren't quite sure it was going to happen. So they quickly gathered all the community together. We all went to the garden. He came and we were all sitting there. We sang songs. He had literally just come from Buckingham Palace to see us.

Jean Vanier died in 2019. I can't remember how we were told. But I remember being invited to the funeral. It was guests only. There were strict instructions not to turn up if you hadn't been invited. It was quite an honour to be invited to such an important funeral. I went with Lucy, our community leader in London, and the community leader from L'Arche Kent. When we came to the funeral we couldn't stay in Trosly, so we stayed in an Airbnb, we did, which had a jacuzzi in the back garden.

We went to the funeral, we did. Lucy and I carried the bread up for the Eucharist. It was an honour to be asked to take part. It was televised around the world, especially in France. People were really sad that Jean had died. There were some important people from France and around the world there. There were over 500 people.

After the funeral, we went back to the Airbnb, took our smart clothes off, put our swimming costumes on and sat in the jacuzzi for about an hour. It was really laid back. We were just lying there with a view of a castle in the background. I think we had some drinks and we kept telling the person next to the switch for bubbles to turn it on again. I enjoyed that very much. We did think this was a bit bad of us after going to a funeral but we all needed it. And enjoyed it!

Revelations of abuse, February 2020

I went to a conference up in Manchester and I had to give a talk with the new National Leader, about L'Arche, I did. So I stood on the stage and I said, '*Oh what a wonderful community L'Arche is and our founder who founded it is such a nice man*'. I found out a week later after this conference, not about the community because the communities are wonderful places, they are, but it is all a pack of lies about the founder, the things that he has done. Because I was told a week later after the conference that the founder – please forgive me because I find it hard to say his name too much now – but I found out a week later about the abuse he did on women. The National Leader already knew about Jean Vanier and there was me rabbiting on about how wonderful he was. I feel a bit of an idiot now that I was saying how wonderful he was when I now know what he did to his victims.

I remember the day I was told the news very well.

It was a Saturday, it was. We should have been all told about it on the Tuesday after but it got leaked, it did, in the press. I remember my community leader, Lucy, phoned me up saying, '*I'm on my way to London now, I am. We're going to have a meeting this afternoon, and please don't put the television on or the radio, not the news*'.

Then I had one of the coordinators phoned me up to come to L'Arche for a meeting in the afternoon. And then I had a telephone call from Laura, the chair of the committee of L'Arche London. She said, '*Oh Richard, could I come to your flat to have a bit of a chat with you?*' I thought, '*Oh crumbs, this is quite serious*'.

Then Laura came to my flat and took me to Hazel's flat. A friend from my church was there already. We all sat down. I thought, '*Oh my God, something big is going on*'. And then Hazel told me what the founder had done. She said that Jean Vanier had abused six ladies who had come to him for spiritual direction. Sadly, he had given a bit more than that. I just want to say the ladies didn't have learning disabilities.

I exploded with anger; I was really f*****g furious. L'Arche seemed a safe place to come to and everyone was caring and treated everyone as equal and there was no scandal or anything – and then, just like an explosion, there **was** scandal in L'Arche and it came from the top, it did. I was frightened and scared and I thought, *'Oh my dear what is this? Where is this all going to end?'* I screamed very loudly and said, *'I'm not safe. No one's safe. Everyone's all the same. I want to leave L'Arche, I do'*.

But then I looked over to Hazel and put my arm around her and said, *'Are you okay Hazel? You knew him. You're not one of the victims are you?'* And she said, *'No'* and we all had a bit of a cry, we did.

Then I asked Hazel, *'Does Christine know about it?'* and she said, *'Yes she does'*. I think I was worried that she was a victim because I knew that Christine and Hazel were quite close to Jean Vanier, in his circle. Christine is the community leader in Trosly and knew Jean.

I just… was quite shocked and upset, and said some things which are quite strong words. And I think I said, *'He couldn't keep it in his pants'*, I said.

I think we all had a bit of a cry about it, we did. Because this was a man who we all looked up to. And some people thought he would be made a saint. But now he'll be known not as a saint, but as an offender.

My mum phoned me and Laura spoke to her and asked her to come up. She did come and had quite a journey to get here but it was good to have her here in the evening.

Laura and I went to Tesco's to get some food and then went up to the community.

Lucy told the news to the community and she said that she came to L'Arche because she wanted to come to the community, not because of the founder. Then I took the microphone, and I think I said, *'He's a f*****g bastard. But what's important is that we need to stay together and to support each other'*. I thought about it, and when I look back at it, I hadn't really heard about the founder before I came to L'Arche, so I like being part of L'Arche because it's a good community and there's a good atmosphere and I like the way they do things, so I decided to stay with the community.

Then I looked across and saw a long-term member of the community, an elderly person in the community, and she was crying. I went across and said to her, *'Are you okay?'* and gave her a cuddle.

When I went home that night I felt a bit numb, a bit angry and a bit sad. I was pleased I had my mum there. She was a good support. She's always a good support, she is.

After hearing what I now know, I wonder what the Queen would think of him now. Even though it's hard to talk about Jean Vanier we do have to remember that he did something wonderful; he set up these wonderful communities. He did give people with learning disabilities the space in the world to do what they can and to be seen.

But how many secrets has he taken to the grave? Because the real bad thing is he denied everything and didn't help the investigations. So where do we go from here? That's the next question now.

CHAPTER 36

COVID

Written 14 December 2020

2020 – What a year it's been! It's been a funny old year, it has. I remember seeing in the new year with my mum and my dad and my brother, Philip, and some friends and their son who is autistic and who doesn't like to have too many people around him. So it just all suits us not to have too much of a big thing, just a quiet celebration. So we all said goodbye to each other when it was all finished, seeing the fireworks on the TV and all that. But I guess this year will be a bit different because we won't be allowed to meet up. We'll all be in our bubbles.

I remember listening to our prime minister Boris Johnson at the start of the first lockdown telling us that we must stay in, just go out to do our exercise, and to stay safe. So everything just closed down. But I also remember just before Boris Johnson made his announcement, the Friday before, we had our Communi-tea (a community gathering each Friday afternoon where there are cups of tea! And we all talk about what we have done over the week and hear what's going to happen the next week), the first time it was done on Zoom. They asked me if I'd like to go up to the community office and to read the information sheet. I remember we were sitting there socially distanced on our chairs. By this time the workshops had all closed, they had. No one was there except me and the assistants. At the end of us doing the information sheet they said that after tonight the office will be closed. I just burst into tears because it just made it all so real, what's going on.

So my key worker changed to having Tim from the office come down to support me. As I understand, Lucy, who is now the community leader, said to the office staff they may need to have to go and support in the houses. So I think Tim volunteered to come and support me.

In the first month of the virus my mum ordered my brother and me a nice food package – a box of a prepared meal with a bottle of wine in it. At Easter she sent a nice hamper of paté and mustard and some nice chutneys for me, and some nice tea biscuits. We phoned each other every day, we did, my mum, my brother and me and my dad was there sitting, he was.

The community were very nice to me too. They sent me materials and stuff so I could join in on activities on Zoom such as paints, pens to colour, paper to draw etc.

People have been very kind to me, people like Jane and my friends from the Lambeth Assembly for people with learning disabilities. We all kept phoning each other every day just to make sure everyone was keeping safe and well.

Hazel phoned me every day. In fact, quite a lot of people checked up on me. It's nice to have people looking out for you, making sure you're okay. And lots of people put messages on Facebook to say thank you for messages I put on there.

The drama group in the community put the story of Aladdin on, we did, and I played the Sultan, I did. We did it on Zoom. We met every week, we did, and we all did our bits in our own flats, we did, some with their support workers and some did it on their own. I did it at my mother's house for the actual performance and my mum helped me to get ready, she did. She found a piece of jewellery for my headdress that she thought would go well. It was fun to do, and quite a challenge to do on Zoom.

I've played many parts at L'Arche and at the Derwen and at Trueloves we did a lot of acting. It is good to do and I do enjoy it. I do like dressing up and looking different from what I usually do. I've been the storyteller in the Nativity Play, a woman in a panto, I've been Jesus, Joseph and I've been the Holy Spirit in dramas!

At Christmas time I couldn't go and spend Christmas as usual with my family, so very kindly a lady from my church who is good friends with the L'Arche community made my Christmas dinner for me and brought it to my flat. So I ate on my own in my flat listening to the Queen. I guess you could say, I toasted the Queen and she toasted me by saying, 'We'll meet again'.

Me dressed as God the Father for a mime at Lambeth Palace, for L'Arche London's 30th anniversary celebrations, 2004

I wrote something for prayers at Communi-tea: my thoughts on isolation.

You get to know yourself better,
and what you find important in life,
what the important things in life are, and the most important is your
family – like my mum and dad, and your brother and nieces and nephew.
People are starting to talk to their neighbours, to get to know them, to
listen to the birds sing.
I saw the other night, I think I saw, Venus up in the sky, the really
bright star.

There are beautiful things happening: you can smell the air, you can see life, animals walking. People are taking an interest in who you are.
Dads are getting to know their children better, helping them with their homework.
I've been painting. My brother played his keyboard for L'Arche Ipswich. You can hear noises, not the usual noises of trains and planes but birds singing.
It's important to keep to your routine but if you don't, that's when trouble starts. You need structure, you do.

My Covid messages on Facebook

Jane suggested to me that perhaps it would be good for me to start putting some messages on Facebook to talk to people in Lambeth. So I did. I think my first message about a thousand people listened to it. The messages were just to reassure people that we were all in this together, not just people with learning disabilities but everybody. I was also keeping contact with my mum and my brother. We were keeping in touch with each other.

So I continued to put my messages on Facebook, I did. Someone said they thought that my messages were better than the prime minister's messages. I noticed on the internet, well I saw a mention of an award that you could nominate people for. I was nominated for this award last year and I said to Jane, perhaps I could nominate someone else for the award. And she said, *'Well you could nominate yourself for the award Richard'.*

I thought, *'That's a bit cheeky, nominating yourself for an award'.* And she said, *'Well, I think it's okay'.* So we put the application in and Jane said, *'We could nominate the messages that you have been putting on Facebook, saying that this is a worldwide pandemic affecting everybody'.*

Both Jane and I received an email to say thank you for my nomination for the award. And they said that they were going to change the awards this year a little bit because of the virus. I could either keep my entry in or I could keep it for next year.

So we kept my entry in, we did, as it was to do with the virus and all that. I got an email to say, *'Congratulations, you have been shortlisted, you have'.* Then a few months later I got an email from Jane to say, *'Did you get an email to say you're one of the winners, you are?'* I said, *'No, I didn't'.* And then Jane said that we had to keep it very quiet. I wasn't allowed to say a word to anyone. So of course I went and told my mum, I did. I told my brother, I did. But then I did keep it quiet for a long while, I did, but it was hard to do because I am not good at keeping secrets!!!

And then about a week before the awards I got an email to say that I could invite some more people to the event if I wanted to. By then I'd told a lot of people so on the evening of the awards I had my support worker with me, Tim from the office who helped me to sort out the technology and stuff to get onto the awards because it was all done by Zoom it was.

The person who was going to present the award to me was Ken Bruce from Radio 2. So we were all there on Zoom. I could see my mum in the corner, I could, I could see my brother, I could see Hazel, I could see Lucy our community leader and others from my community. All there to support me, which was nice.

So I got the award virtually, I did, as it was all on Zoom. It's the Learning Disability and Autism Leaders' List award. I think this means I am now a Learning Disability Leader but to be truthful I'm not too sure. I've since found out that someone from another L'Arche community got the same award a few years ago.

They announced our names and showed a clip of us, all the winners, what we had done and all that. So people saw our stories, they did, all the winners. And after the ceremony I found out that I had lots of messages on Twitter saying, '*Well done Richard!*' People who had heard of me. Even my local MP, Helen Hayes, tweeted and said, '*Well done Richard!*'

Now people are saying I am now a national leader, not just a local leader. A few days ago I had an email from Heather of L'Arche UK who wanted to write a piece about me for the L'Arche UK national newsletter or something. She said, '*I just want to go over a few things with you to make sure I get everything right in the piece*'. Basically she said I have so many titles now she couldn't write them all down. So we had a bit of a joke about that, we did. I guess that's a good way of ending writing about Covid. There is light at the end of the tunnel now, I think.

CHAPTER 37

MY NAME ON THE DOOR

I started my job with Irene at Kingston University in January 2021. A few years ago, I did a research course with Irene, I did, about how to do research. After we did the eight-week course, she said that she was hoping to get some funding for a job to employ a person with a learning disability to help her do some research. She asked me if I would like to apply for the job, but I think she asked everyone with a learning disability in her network if they would want to apply; it wasn't just me.

So, in December 2020, I saw the job application for the job and so I applied for the job, I did. And I was lucky enough to get an interview. So I had the interview, I did. I was all dressed up smart; I was looking at the computer screen having an interview on Zoom. It was a bit strange, it was. After the interview Irene said to me, '*Thank you very much Richard. We will let you know by the end of the week, but it might be by the end of the day*'.

In the afternoon I had to do another job for somebody, I did. While I was doing that the telephone rang. Irene had called me to say, '*Congratulations Richard! You got the job on the "Growing Older" project*'. I said, '*Thank you very much Irene*'. I felt quite excited. It was nice to get a proper job where I would get paid at the end of the month. It's quite a big thing for me, it is. I now have a proper ID card to get into the university, I have. It's quite exciting. It makes you feel important to have an ID card to get into the research offices where I work. I can even go into the staff canteen now, I can.

So I started my job working with Irene. It's all been done on computer, it has, because of Covid so it's all been a bit weird. But I did properly meet the team, I did. There's Irene the professor, Becky the doctor who I'll be working with mostly on the research, and me the research assistant. Irene said, '*The first thing we've got to do is to employ someone who can support you Richard in doing your job*'. Irene said to me that usually the first thing she would do is to welcome us in the office with a cup of coffee (but I only like tea to drink), and some chocolate I think, she said.

Me and the team (L to R: Irene, Richard, Jo, Becky) on my first day in the office, June 2021

Becky said to me, 'We've got some forms to fill out first before we can properly get started'. So we did all the paperwork. We ended up doing the interviews to find someone to help me with the job. We found a nice woman called Jo. We have given ourselves a name now, we have. We're the A-Team, we are!

We started to meet a few people who were helping us to do our research. And we started the bigger team who are also on the project we are doing. So I've been working there for a while now. I went to the Oval Cricket Ground to talk to all the other people who work at the university in Irene's department. They were having an away day, they were. And I told them about the project we are doing, about people with learning disabilities who are getting old but are still living with their families. We ask them about their plans for the future after their mums and dads are sadly not here anymore. We've been busy doing interviews with people with learning disabilities aged about 40 or 50 who are still living with their families.

Because of circumstances, Jo, my support worker, her son had to self-isolate so she couldn't come as she was self-isolating for ten days. Irene was in Holland, she was, and Becky was on holiday. So I had to do it my own, I did. We did prepare a short presentation by video to show them. But the Vice Dean felt sorry for me, so they made arrangements for me to go to the Oval on my own in a taxi to give the presentation. I was a bit nervous about giving the talk but I got good feedback after giving the talk and everyone said, *'Thank you very much'*. And to top it all off, I got there, but rain had stopped play so I didn't get to see any cricket.

I think that the icing on the cake in my new job was being asked to be interviewed on the *BBC News* and seeing my name on the news with the title, Research Assistant. I was being interviewed about Covid and the vaccinations. Jo Whiley, who is a presenter on Radio 2, had been offered a vaccine before her sister who has a learning disability, who lives in a care home. They wanted to speak to an expert about it, so I also featured on the news report with Jo Whiley talking about people with learning disabilities who should be offered the vaccine in care homes. We were interviewed by Nikki Fox. In the end the government did a U turn, they did. I felt quite good that I helped to get the government to do a U turn!

Irene told me I had passed my probation and so I am now a full member of the university team. I'd like to help Irene and her team to see that people with learning disabilities can help with big decisions and work in research. She's a lovely lady to work with. She makes you feel welcome and part of the team. She makes the work fun, she does. We always have a chocolate biscuit and a cup of tea or something.

I remember the first time I went in to do my job in the office at the hospital, Jo and me went into the office on our own and did a bit of investigating around the place so we could get our bearings and all that. We were given instructions about what to do from Irene and Becky. When we got to Irene's office there was a nice card in her office for me saying, *'Welcome Richard!'* and two boxes of chocolates, one for me and one for Jo, to say, *'You made it!'*

And then I looked at the door. It had Professor Irene Tuffrey-Wijne's Office on it, and underneath it, *'Richard Keagan-Bull: Research Assistant'*. So I thought, *'I've really made it. My name on the door!'*

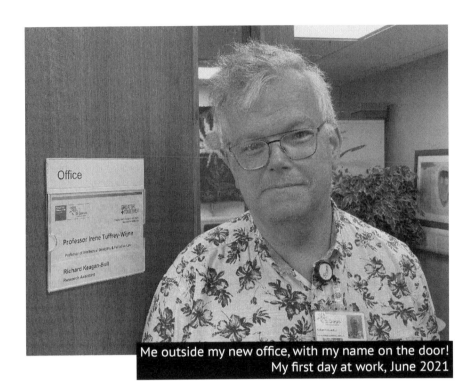

Me outside my new office, with my name on the door!
My first day at work, June 2021

CHAPTER 38

CONCLUDING THOUGHTS

I wanted to write my life story to have a sort of diary and to remember the things what I have done in my past and what I have achieved. At some point, people can look at my life story and remember things what have happened and hopefully in some of it, it might make people think, and maybe cry in some bits, but also they might also have a jolly good laugh over a cup of tea over some of the things what I did.

I want people to say about my life, he used to make us laugh, he did. Sometimes he could be a bit annoying, a bit of a nuisance, but most of the time he had a good sense of humour, he did, and he could light a room up. My gift is that I can stand up for people with learning disabilities who are less able than me and say how it is. And I can look back at being the founding chair of the National Speaking Group for L'Arche UK and also one of the founding chairs in Lambeth of the Assembly Meeting for people with learning disabilities.

And when people come to visit me in my flat, they do go, 'Wow!' at some of the things what I have done and made.

My message to society is, firstly, it's me who's got the learning disability. Secondly, if I was to shake your hand, you couldn't catch my learning disability from me. It's not a disease you can catch.

The things what I have achieved in my life are firstly done with some paid support from organisations like L'Arche, some with care and love from my mum and my family, but most of all it's me who has to get out of bed in the morning and stand up and do the things what I have learnt to do, and now I can stand in front of big crowds and tell the people that people with learning disabilities are able to do things, maybe not as fast and as quick as an able-bodied person but we do have the right to be listened to and to be understood and to take part in society.

Me and my mum

The gift of people with learning disabilities is their way of seeing things. Maybe they don't see exactly the way others see, and sometimes the only way they can express themselves is by getting upset and anxious, or they can give you cuddles, they can. They often are the ones who see when someone is sad and lonely, and they are the ones who can be the comforter. Sometimes you have to look into the eyes of the person to get to know them, and just to hold their hands sometimes to make them feel safe and secure.

I hope that whoever reads this book or my story will look at it and tell their friends, *'This man has taken part in normal activities and has spoken out for people with learning disabilities and his voice should be heard and listened to'.*

And that's why I've named the book ***Don't put us away!***

POSTSCRIPT BY RICHARD'S SECRETARY

Clotted cream tea in Hazel's garden

I can't remember if it was Richard's idea to write his life story or whether I suggested it. He was certainly keen. My job was simply to type what Richard said. Each week he would turn up clear about what he wanted to say and very chronological in the order of his memories. Often I had to ask him to slow down as I could hardly keep up with his flow of thought. I tried hard to write down exactly what I heard. Of course, I knew nothing of his life before L'Arche. I was moved by parts of his story, and in the chapter on the tin of peaches I was almost weeping with laughter as I tried to keep typing!

Once Richard had almost finished he began to look more seriously at publishing his story. This meant editing the work done so far. Here certain details and names were changed to protect people's identity. Elsewhere permission was sought to include people's names or photos.

In the editing I added in certain clarifying details. I also occasionally probed with a few questions to elicit more details for clarity but what is typed are Richard's memories and words. The writing took a few years due to my other commitments and Richard's travels. This meant changing some tenses to the past as we edited his story.

One Friday towards the end of the writing of Richard's life story, he phoned me. *'Will you be at home on Tuesday?'* to which I replied, *'Yes'*.

'Then keep an eye out!'

Then on the Monday he phoned and said, *'Will you be in between 10.30 and 12.30 tomorrow?'* to which I replied, *'Yes'*.

'Then keep an eye out!'

The next day there was a ring at the door. I opened it to see a delivery man with a very large and heavy box for me. When I opened it, I discovered four scones, four pots of clotted cream, four pots of strawberry jam, brownies, flapjacks, lemon drizzle cake, carrot cake. Far too much for me to eat on my own, and such good food needed to be enjoyed fresh! So I phoned Richard and invited him for afternoon tea in my garden with my best bone china. I know his taste and love of quality things! It was such a thoughtful generous gift.

Richard knows how to enjoy life, how to be generous, how to be grateful, how to create community, how to be faithful as a friend. Our afternoon tea party was typical of Richard – and fun!

It was a privilege and fun to work for Richard. I hope people enjoy his story as much as he has enjoyed his life!

Hazel Bradley

REFERENCES

Derwen College: www.derwen.ac.uk

L'Arche UK: www.larche.org.uk

Walsingham Support: www.walsingham.com

Mabel Cooper's life story: www.open.ac.uk/health-and-social-care/research/shld/resources-and-publications/life-stories/mabels-story

Prof Irene Tuffrey-Wijne's research at Kingston University: www.tuffrey-wijne.com/?page_id=51

Templeton Prize: www.templetonprize.org/templeton-prize-history/

INDEX